Tree: Essence

CW00833277

Simon & Sue Lilly

Tree: Essence of Healing

Cover design by Paul Mason
Internal illustrations by Simon & Sue Lilly

Published by:

Capall Bann Publishing
Freshfields
Chieveley
Berks
RG20 8TF

Dedicated to Ögyen Menla.

Om a hung bendzra guru bekanse maha bekanse siddhi
bekanse hung bekanse a hung a.

By the same authors, also published by Capall Bann:

Crystal Doorways
Tree: Essence, Spirit and Teacher
Tree Seer

Contents

Preface   1
Introduction   3
Tree Essences   **8**
    The Memory of Water   10
    Flower Energy   11
    Making an Essence   12
    Alternate Methods of Making Essences   18
    Using Essences   20
    How to Use Essences   22
    Aura Sweep   24
    Essence Inhalation   25
    Bathing   25
    Spraying Essences   25
The Chakras   **27**
    Base Chakra   29
    Second, Sacral Chakra   29
    Solar Plexus Chakra   30
    Heart Chakra   31
    Throat Chakra   31
    Brow Chakra   32
    Crown Chakra   33
    Using Essences With Chakras   34
Subtle Bodies   **35**
    The Etheric Body   36
    The Emotional Body   36
    The Mental Body   37
    The Astral Body   38
The Meridian System   **40**
    The Meridians, Their End-Points and Emotional
               Connotations   41
    Central Meridian (Conception Vessel)   41
    Governing Vessel   41
    Gall Bladder Meridian   42
    Liver Meridian   42

Bladder Meridian 42
Kidney Meridian 42
Large Intestine (Colon) Meridian 42
Lung Meridian 42
Stomach Meridian 43
Spleen Meridian 43
Circulation-Sex Meridian (Pericardium, Heart
Protector) 43
Triple Warmer Meridian (Triple Heater) 43
Heart Meridian 43
Small Intestine Meridian 44
Meridian Massage 44
Essences and the Meridian System 45
Using Acupuncture Points 46
Trees For Healing **48**
Pathways of Acquiescence 51
Healing the whole or healing the bits 53
In the Presence of Trees 55
Standing Like a Tree 55
Energy Signatures 57
Symptomatic versus Constitutional 59
Plant Spirit Healing 60
The Spirit of Cherry 61
Spirit Medicine 63
Asking for Help 65
HEALING TREES **67**
Alder 69
Apple 73
Ash 77
Bay 81
Beech 83
Bird Cherry 87
Black Poplar 89
Blackthorn 93
Box 95
Catalpa 99
Cedar of Lebanon 101
Cherry Laurel 103

Cherry Plum	107
Copper Beech	111
Crack Willow	113
Elder	117
English Elm	119
Field Maple	123
Gean (Wild Cherry)	125
Giant Redwood (Giant Sequoia, Wellingtonia)	129
Glastonbury Thorn	131
Gorse	135
Great Sallow	137
Hawthorn	141
Hazel	143
Holly	147
Holm Oak	149
Hornbeam	153
Horse Chestnut	155
Italian Alder	159
Ivy	161
Judas Tree	163
Laburnum	167
Larch	169
Lawson Cypress	171
Leyland Cypress	175
Lilac	179
Lime	181
Lucombe Oak	185
Magnolia	187
Manna Ash	191
Medlar	193
Mimosa	197
Midland Hawthorn	199
Monkey Puzzle Tree	203
Monterey Pine	205
Mulberry	209
Norway Maple	211
Oak	213
Osier	219

Pear   221
Persian Ironwood   223
Plane Tree   227
Plum   229
Pittespora   233
Privet   235
Red Chestnut   239
Red Oak   241
Rowan   245
Scots Pine   247
Silver Birch   251
Silver Maple   255
Spindle   259
Stag's Horn Sumach   261
Strawberry Tree   263
Sweet Chestnut   267
Sycamore   271
Tamarisk   275
Tree Lichen   279
Tree of Heaven   281
Tulip Tree   285
Viburnum   287
Wayfaring Tree   291
Weeping Willow   293
Whitebeam   297
White Poplar   299
White Willow   303
Wych Elm   305
Yellow Buckeye   309
Yew   311
Index   **312**

Preface

This is the second volume in a series exploring the spiritual nature of the Tree Kingdoms. Volume One, *"Tree: Essence, Spirit and Teacher"* concentrates on practical ways to interact with the spiritual reality of trees. Volume Two, looks at ways that tree energy may be of use in situations where healing is required. In large part it focuses on the energy characteristics of trees that the authors have discovered in their development of "Green Man Tree Essences"

As such, this present volume provides flower essence therapists and other users with the fullest explanation to date of this range. However, the information offered here can be of use to anyone who wishes to expand their perception of the potential of the Tree Kingdoms and is not tied to any single product, point-of-view or belief system.

Although the information presented here is often quite detailed and specific, the reader is asked to treat everything as a clue rather than concrete fact. The authors are quite willing to be proved wrong in their analyses if it means that more people have been encouraged to explore the Tree Kingdoms for themselves. Each tree species and its enlivening spirit is a whole world not easily encapsulated or defined in a few words. The roads down which we have been led, may for others, turn out to be "cul-de-sacs" or red herrings. It is our hope that others will find their own roads with the guiding awareness of the tree spirits themselves. For clarity, some information has been included here from Volume One, particularly the discussion on essences and how they can be used.

Introduction

It was a chance remark by a student of ours that gave us the idea of tree essences. We had begun to make flower essences using the traditional methods when we moved into the Devon countryside outside Exeter. On the few sunny days that first spring and summer we would collect various garden and hedgerow flowers and place them in bowls of clear water for several hours, until the water became charged with the vibration of the plant. It was then filtered and bottled with brandy as a preservative, and stored to await assessment of its properties.

All this was a fairly random procedure - what took our eye or what we were curious about. We knew of several other collections that used British plants and there were numerous selections from more fashionable and exotic locations with an enormous range of species. It was difficult to envisage a definitive collection of British flower essences that would take less than a lifetime to accumulate or that didn't repeat essences made by others in the field. It would be much more suitable and satisfying to limit our attentions in some way. Talking about essences at the end of lecture one evening, someone said, "Oh, I'd love to try Hazel!" and that was it. Tree essences.

Although some tree essences have been used for years, particularly those originally identified by Dr. Edward Bach (1886 - 1936), and a few that appear in other collections, there was not, to our knowledge, a comprehensive collection of native British tree essences. As it was February at the time we had that spring and summer to begin work. Consulting various tree books we compiled a calendar for collecting flowers. It was going to be very busy in April and May, gradually quietening down with just the occasional collection in the late summer and autumn. Hazel was already in full flower along our lanes and this was the first essence we made - very appropriate as Hazel encourages the growth of new skills, new information and focus of mind.

As the weeks went by we collected more essences and began finding ways of solving new problems. Finding and identifying trees was just a matter of practice, but the actual collection of flowers was not always straightforward. Finding a tree in full flower on a sunny day in a fairly quiet spot often led to the frustration of not being able to reach the blossoms! Once we had seen that one species was beginning to flower it was a question of running round keeping an eye open for a reachable branch.

Few of us notice the varied and seasonal appearance of tree flowers because, apart from a few exceptions like horse chestnut and the fruit trees, many are small and inconspicuous. However, once you begin to take notice it is a wonder how you ever managed to ignore what was going on up above our heads.

Humanity's relationship with trees is as old as life itself. They are, at the most fundamental level, the cause and the sustainer of our reality. Climate, atmospheric composition, geology and the formation of life on this planet is largely due to green plants and trees in particular. They are the only means by which sunlight can be turned into matter and energy; they absorb and distribute minerals otherwise locked in the soil and rock so that it becomes a stable sustainer of life maintaining nutrient balance and water moisture; they create and maintain a viable atmosphere by locking up carbon dioxide in organic compounds whilst releasing oxygen into the air; they release water vapour which fuels the water cycle.

It is really only in the last fifty years that the expansion of the petrochemical industry has begun to replace trees as our main resource. Buildings, furniture, tools, vehicles all relied on the versatility and flexibility of wood. Heat, light, food, shelter,

4

protection - all proceeded from trees and tree products. However much we may now replace wood with plastic or metals, the underlying fact is still that without the tree we cannot maintain our existence in this world. So why is it that most of us walk past the largest organism we are likely to meet in our everyday lives, beings to whom we owe our very existence, and pay as little attention to them as if they were chipboard wardrobes?

Even whilst they were mankind's major resource, trees were also revered and cared for as sacred and magical beings. It is not by chance that the tree appears so often as a central symbol in cosmologies, especially as the sustainer, the nurturer, the first or original home, the means to reach other levels of existence, the means to redemption and so on.

A tree cannot choose its place of growth. It can only survive and flourish by adjusting its form to harmonise with the prevailing conditions. The very fact that a tree grows up, matures, flowers and bears fruit means that it has succeeded in maintaining the balance for tens, hundreds or even thousands of years. It is this ability to remain balanced and flexible, to absorb and let go, to just remain harmless that is so often transferred to tree essences.

Each species shows different habits and characteristics which are the outward, visible manifestation of the energy with which they are formed. It is the pattern of this energy that is imprinted on water molecules in the process of preparing the essences. This is why the ancient "Doctrine of Signatures" can still be relevant in identifying the properties a particular tree has. The "Doctrine" simply recognises that the outward form reflects the inner energies (as a crystal's shape is determined by the energy patterns of its constituent atoms), and that a symbolic link, whether that be shape or colour or habit, is a link nonetheless, and will create a resonance in a similar structure or pattern within us. When our tree essences have been assessed to find out their properties it is interesting to look back at the physical characteristics, folklore and traditions. Very often it is possible to see a unifying thread of experience running through all the diverse sources.

One thing we wanted to emphasise with our tree essences was that they are not just another alternative to reach for when disease symptoms pop up, like an etheric or spiritual aspirin! Although they have proved to be very effective healing tools for deep level healing, we hope that they also provide a means to get back into constructive relationship with tree energies. This is why the range of essences is called "Green Man Tree Essences". The image of the Green Man is the perfect blending of human and plant features represented for centuries in churches and cathedrals as the ever-present power of Nature and the mysterious awareness of a viewpoint beyond human time and space. Perhaps the closest we may now come to defining that sense of mystery for ourselves is to walk alone into an ancient woodland or forest where, after a little while, we begin to feel a difference, a sense of otherness all around us. By integrating the vibration of trees into our own energy systems we can, perhaps, begin to understand a larger view of life, and behave with more maturity and consideration as co-creators of our world.

The "active ingredient" of vibrational essences is the vibration or energy pattern itself, which is essentially non-physical. Because they stimulate the subtle energy fields it is only necessary to bring the tree essence into the aura for it to start working. For example: a few drops can be added to bathwater or to a massage oil. It can be placed on the wrist pulses, forehead, soles of the feet or on meridian or acupuncture points. They can be mixed with a little water, put in a plant sprayer or atomiser, them sprayed around a body or in a room. This is an instantaneous way of infusing a new energy into an environment and is like walking into a grove of your favourite trees! We have heard of a meditation group who place a bowl of water tree essence in their room. Each person on entering rubs a little of the water on their hands and then passes them around the body so that the vibration of the tree enters their auric field. In this way the whole group energy becomes coherent and has a direct link to the tree and its characteristic properties. For example, were Strawberry Tree to be used, a deep level of stillness would be experienced, the crown chakra would be stimulated and changes would be more likely to occur at fundamental levels of the self.

Using a tree essence is a quick way to link our subtle selves to the natural world and we hope it will foster a deeper awareness of our inter-relatedness and of the unity of all life. As so much disease and illness begins from a blocking of life-force within us, or from denial of some part of existence, it is no wonder that tree essences can be of use in the healing process and in the deepening of meditation experiences and self-discovery.

Tree Essences

In our work with trees and tree spirits we have found the use of tree essences invaluable. They are, for us, one of the primary keys to open awareness to the Tree Kingdoms. Through an essence we can instantly access the energy signature, the feel, the presence and the awareness-being of a particular type of tree. The whole environment can be imbued with this energy and we can immerse ourselves within it.

With the physical presence of a tree - no matter how sentient or how powerful, it is difficult for many of us to quickly go beyond the constant awareness of "selfness" that immediately creates a subject-object relationship. This can then create a divide between ourselves and the spirit worlds. We are used to our physical existence, the presence of our bodies and of being "inside" them. We are always looking out, and so we are separated from the world. What is "out there" is the realm of our five senses and if we begin to perceive or understand something not through our sense organs it is very easy to doubt the experience. It can very easily become "only our imagination".

Using tree essences we can help to remove this perceptual and intellectual barrier. Not only can we "step into" the energy of a tree, for instance when the essence is sprayed around a room, but the tree energy can directly enter into us if a few drops are taken by mouth, or rubbed onto pulse points. In other words, using the tree essence helps to amplify the experience of the characteristic feel of a tree.

Not only do we perceive with our external senses the quality of a physical tree, but we activate all our internal senses as well- those feelings and body wisdom mechanisms that in everyday, externalised life we tend to ignore.

There seems to be no clear evidence from the past of the use of flower essences as we know them today, though there are similar, subtle techniques described in a wider cultural context. The most apparent seems to be the collection of morning dew, off flowers and leaves, recorded in medieval European magical traditions. Paracelsus in the 16th century is reputed to have done so to heal emotional imbalances in his patients. As he was the primary synthesiser of Classical and native (pagan) healing and spiritual techniques, it is reasonable to assume that he was borrowing from established traditions. When Dr. Edward Bach first began his experiments with flower energies in the 1920's he seems to have combined the magical dew-collecting of Paracelsus with the theoretical background of homoeopathy. With direct personal intuitive insights he began by roaming the countryside at dawn collecting and drinking the dew off certain plants. For practical reasons he developed other collecting and preparation techniques that are still in use today.

Among the native peoples of the world, flowers and plants are the primary source of healing and spiritual energies. As the power of the plant comes from its spirit, many cultures will include preparations from the required plants by making broths, baths, bundles, oils, tinctures and so on, to be administered externally or internally. The chemical properties of the plant may or may not be employed in a conscious manner - the spirit is all-important. We shall see that in modern flower essence usage, subtracting all the jargon and pseudo-scientific terminology, it also comes back to the same thing: the intangible, indefinable, unmeasurable spirit of the plant. So what is a flower essence?

A flower essence is an energy signature of a plant held in water, usually preserved in brandy or another alcohol. Orthodox testing would reveal nothing other than water and brandy - there is no physical presence of the plant at all, and in this flower essences differ from that other more well-known energy medicine: homoeopathy, in which at lower potencies there can still be found minute amounts of original material.

Just about the only tangible evidence of some subtle change in state can be revealed by taking a Kirlian photograph of an essence droplet and comparing it to other essences and simple water or alcohol. The energy discharge from an essence is immediately recognisable by its dynamism and corona. The most sensitive apparatus available to us is our own body, and it is on this that the essences can have immediate and profound results.

The Memory of Water

In attempting to refute the efficacy of homoeopathic medical practices a French scientist, Jacques Benveniste, not only found that homoeopathic principles are sound but that the primary mechanism for their function is in the nature of water itself. The bonding between hydrogen and oxygen atoms is remarkably flexible and the angles can vary more than with any other known substance. The theory goes that by this means water carries a "memory" of what it has been in contact with, carried in the atomic structure itself. This is sufficient to transfer the energy patterns to other systems like the human being, and by some resonant process alter the energy configurations by a completely non-physical means. For his startling, exact and paradigm-shifting work, Benveniste was of course immediately vilified and unceremoniously thrown out of the orthodox consensus scientific community. There is nothing scientists dislike more than a smart-ass who comes up with a new idea to upset the neat hypotheses of The Real World.

Until the last few years, when new techniques have been tried out, flower essences were largely made by the sun-water method. Flowers were collected and floated in a plain bowl of spring water for several hours in bright sunlight. The resulting charged water was then bottled with alcohol as a preservative. Nothing much could be simpler! This seems to be sufficient in nearly every case to infuse the water with some quality from the plant. The full procedure will be examined shortly, but first of all: why flowers?

Flower Energy

If it is the signature of the entire plant that becomes integrated into the structure of the water, then why are the flowers the parts so often used? It is true that nowadays essences are being made from all parts of plants from root to seed and all are effective. It may be that there are slightly different emphases to an essence made from a root, a leaf, a seed. In general, it is the flower that is most commonly used to make an essence. If we think of our appreciation-where our attention travels to-whole businesses are built on this attraction to the shape, colour and smell of flowers. Of all the parts of a plant, the flower is the most specifically created to interact with its environment. The flower is the communication vehicle of a plant. It is there to be noticed, to be smelled, to be crawled into, to be sucked, to be pollinated by something of another realm-be that insect, bird, animal or the wind and rain. The peculiar structure of each flower acknowledges the many mechanisms of the outer world, the "not-I". It is this interaction with the "not-I" upon which the continuation of the plant and its species ultimately depends. This outwards expression of the life-force of the plants is thus perceived by us as being the powerful culmination of growth, of manifestation, of individuality, of self-awareness. Our emotions are almost automatically and immediately affected by the colour, smell and shape of a flower in a way that a leaf or stem fails to achieve. The immediate appreciation of a flower that we as humans feel, the aesthetic of the sense perceptions, shows us a biological reality. Flowers are biologically important for our survival.

The flower is like a psychic head, eye, voice and message drawing our attention and holding us in focused but free-floating contemplation. With such a deep-felt contact, carefully picking a few flower heads, placing them on water and treating them as reverential offerings from another Kingdom-the message and the messenger-is a natural ritual interaction.

From another perspective the flower is the most ephemeral expression of the energy of the whole plant and its removal will not, in most cases, permanently damage the plant.

Making an Essence

If you want to make an essence, begin by using the most straightforward sun and water method. Once familiar with this you will be more confident to modify and try other approaches.

Get a plain glass bowl that, if possible, is free of all patterns, names and numbers. Each of these will carry another vibration so it is best to avoid confusing your essence. Some better class of glassware has removable labels and inexpensive dessert bowls are often free from stamping. If you are thinking of making a few essences, you may want to have bowls of different sizes. This is because it is thought best to cover the whole surface of the water with flowers and, while some flowers are quite large, others, including a lot of tree flowers, are very small.

You will need to fill this bowl with as pure a water as possible. Spring water is the best, direct from the source or else use a good quality bottled water. It is not really possible to avoid pollutants these days, even ground water may have high levels of chemical fertiliser.

It is best to make essences only of those plants that attract your attention, that draw you in some way to them. These are plants to which you have some significant link at that time so you will automatically be more in tune with their energy patterns.

Spend some time familiarising yourself with the tree or plant. This doesn't necessarily mean sitting for hours boring the spirits with doe-eyed mood-making, unless you like that sort of thing. It is best to have some heart connection with the plant's presence, but it is very unlikely that you will have no empathy or you would have little interest in this sort of thing in the first place.

If the essence is to be of a tree flower and you know the attunement techniques, (See *Tree: Essence, Spirit and Teacher.* Volume One) you can use some to create an even flow of energy between you.

When you feel comfortable with the plant's presence (this may be almost immediate or can be a slow growth of appreciative awareness over a week or two), it is a good idea to verbally or mentally explain what you are going to do and for what reasons. Also ask permission to take flowers from the plant. The emotional intent of harmlessness and sensitivity is very obvious to plant awareness so coherent framing of thought is more important for your own clarity of purpose than to the plant. Clarity of thought may also help you to focus your emotional/feeling stance.

When you ask for permission it is important to quieten your mind and listen or feel for a response. This you might perceive as an inner voice or as a change of emotional pressure, either relaxing or tensing. If you feel resistance in some way, ask again and if the feeling remains the same move to another plant or try again some other time. If communication is good you might try asking what is the reason for the refusal. Sometimes it can be just a simple question of etiquette, or you may need to perform some small ritual act to get into a more appropriate state of mind. If it is the tree itself that is unwilling to participate, finding out why can sometimes allow you to help by offering healing. A genuine offering of assistance is never wasted-even though you might have to modulate your thought patterns to elicit a useful response. Some tree spirits can be very tetchy if they have suffered in the past from lack of care or are unwell.

When you have felt the positive response to your request for a few flowers, you can go about carefully collecting them. If possible it is a good idea to collect flowers from different parts of the tree or from different nearby trees. What you are able to reach will somewhat limit this choice as not all trees put out flowers near to the ground. Looking out for trees growing on slopes where more of the mature branches can be reached, has become for us an automatic pastime. How you pick the flowers is up to you and you will need to experiment with different methods until you find one that is comfortable for you. I find that different trees require different techniques simply because of the physical diversity of flowers. Some are easy to pinch off without crushing them using a pair of silver sugar tongs, others need more dextrous fingers and sharp nails to gather. Many tree flowers are very small and you will need a degree of focused patience and a relatively small bowl.

As you collect the flowers place them carefully on the surface of the water. When there are enough to cover the surface leave the bowl in full sun close to the plant. Sometimes it will not be possible to leave the bowl, so if this is the case just place the bowl on some kind of natural surface, such as wood or stone (try to avoid the strong unnatural vibration of metal, plastic or concrete).

Take care where you place the bowl. What starts off in full sun, may in a short time be in deep shade and this will lengthen the energising process. Also, if you are leaving the bowl for any length of time be aware of the possibility that it will be found by domestic animals-thirsty dogs and curious cats can demolish a day's work in a flash, so place the bowl high enough off the ground.

The length of time it takes to energise the water is very variable. Different essence-makers use many different rules and regulations, but what is laid down in one book may not be the most useful technique for you to use. So much depends on the conditions when the essence is being made. Classically, the optimal time for essence-making is in the early morning in spring or summertime on a cloudless, sunny day. In these

14

conditions two or three hours is often cited as being sufficient to potentise the water. Since many books on essences are written by Americans who live on the West Coast of the USA, adverse weather conditions are rarely considered. Compared to the British Isles, southern California has no weather: when the sun is not shining, it is night-time!

Clouds, six different climates in an hour, and startlingly short flowering periods coinciding with weeks of continuous rain - this is the norm for the British essence maker. It has the tendency to create jumpy, nervous individuals who continually glance from bud to sky to bud again, but it also creates flexibility, opportunism and new ways of working. The only rule you need in essence making is: do what is appropriate at the time, according to your insight. So in conditions that are less than ideal, when there is cloud cover, or if you expect sunshine and showers between thunderstorms, allow longer exposure of the essence to sunlight. In really dull conditions you might consider putting the bowl on a mirror surface to reflect the light. On rainy days cover the bowl with a sheet of glass or a larger bowl to prevent swamping with rain water. Use your imagination and experiment. If you have been inspired to make an essence at a certain time make it then. It will be the most powerful for you whatever the conditions.

It is important whenever possible to use flowers that are in full bloom and undamaged. This very often means carefully watching your chosen tree for the best time to prepare the essence. You will find that trees of the same species will flower at different times depending on their age and where they are situated. If you find your tree has already passed its peak and is dropping petals, look around for another tree that has slightly later flowering. Remember that different parts of the same tree will often be ahead or behind the rest in its growth cycle depending whether it is in sun or shade.

If you don't have a testing skill like dowsing or muscle-testing you will have to rely more on the rules, or else quieten yourself and ask your deep mind or intuition to let you know when the essence "feels" ready to bottle.

Essences made at any time of year except very early in spring or late autumn will tend to accumulate at least a few insects, as well as wind-blown sticks and leaves. These will have to be lifted out of the water together with the flowers. What you do with these flowers is up to you, but it is important to treat them with care and consideration. They can be dried to use as a basis for incense, offerings, herb bundles; placed in another decorative bowl as an indoor display until they fade; placed back under the trees you have gathered from; put on the soil or in compost to continue the cycle of life. Whatever you do, do it with awareness and thanks. Some authors suggest a twig or leaf of the plant is used to lift the flowers off the water. Try it and see: sometimes it works, sometimes it is worse than those annoying Christmas toys with ball bearings that have to be jiggled into place simultaneously. Avoid frustration if at all possible. It is a strong projecting emotion and can interfere with the quality of your essence. A small silver spoon or silver sugar tongs are quite versatile and silver is a fairly benign, neutral metal to use.

Once the flowers and larger bugs are removed it is a good idea to filter out smaller particles of flower, pollen and creepy-crawlies. Using another clean glass vessel strain the water through a fine cheesecloth, linen or filter paper. This will help to prevent any fungal or bacterial growth in the essence bottle.

Most essence makers use a spirit like brandy or vodka for a preservative. If alcohol is a problem, a vinegar will preserve equally effectively, though the smell and taste tends to linger long after the alcohol would have evaporated. Fill the storage bottle at least half-full with the preservative and then top up with the potentised water. Give the mix a good shake to help the stabilisation of the energies. This is the mother essence. Clearly label and date it. Most essence makers will keep the mother essence as the primary source and will use the dilution commonly called the stock bottle. Stock is made by taking a few drops, usually between three and seven, from the mother essence and putting them in another bottle containing at least fifty percent brandy and topped up with water.

Whether you use the mother essence or the stock essence (or even the next dilution down-the "dosage" level where drops are taken from the "stock" and placed in another bottle of water/brandy), will depend on how much essence was originally made and how frequently it is going to be used.

Each essence maker seems to have their own ideas concerning the efficacy of the different levels of dilution. I suspect most are adhering to a set of personal belief-systems with which they feel comfortable (and therefore effective in their own experience), rather than there being one ineffable law of nature entitled: "Essences and the Uses Thereof." We return to the original perplexity. What is it that comprises an essence? If it is essentially a physical process then it should be able to be measured in some way. If it is not a physical process then the rules of mass, weight, proportion, location in time and space, and other means of measuring the "amount" of essence present in any one bottle cannot apply. If this is so, then how can one "dilute" a vibration (with no mass etc.)? It is either there or not there . It is difficult to conceive of an energy pattern that is "not-there-very-much".

Being human, however, measurement, the process and the recipe - all the ritual of creating and passing on information and knowledge-is very important to most of us. Following instructions means that we know when we are "right" and when we have done it "wrong". Doing the same thing as someone else who has got a good result makes us happier to encourage a similar outcome, and so it will tend to happen that way. "Take three drops, four times a day and you will get better" is what the majority of us want to hear. We don't want to be reminded of self-responsibility and self-determination. Most of us haven't been trained to really understand what they mean. "Do as you're told" has been endlessly reinforced through the long years of schooling. "Do what you think is best" is only considered the precursor of avoiding or attributing blame. by someone else.

Alternate Methods of Making Essences
It is well worth making a few tree essences for yourself, firstly to establish the ease of the process and, secondly, to experience the nuances and shifts of awareness that occur during the whole time. There is a particular state that soon descends as one goes out with the intention to make a flower essence very close to meditative states and the heightened awareness achieved during extended retreats. The simplicity and tried and tested efficacy of the traditional sun-water method should be used first of all.

Over the years new methods have evolved that seem to prove equally effective and provide solutions in instances where the sun-water method may be inappropriate. These new techniques slide effortlessly away from any pseudo-scientifically justifiable procedures and simply become magical invocation and evocation.

The first essence maker Edward Bach was flexible in his approach. Although the sun-water technique arose from the early dew-drinking phase, a good proportion of his flower essences were prepared by boiling. Now boiling, can, in no way, be understood as a simple vibrational technique. The result will always be a herbal infusion or tisane of some concentration. It could be argued that the energy signature is also present in the water, but there will be quite a physical molecular presence as well. And what can be said of the remedy Rock Water? Rock Water is exactly what it says it is - water collected from mountain streams running through and over native rock. It does what it says but there is not a flower in sight. Today there are an increasing number of such "environmental essences" that have been made to capture a particular time or place.

There are essences of locations, equinoxes, sacred sites, specific types of environments, sea creatures, dolphins, whales, planets and stars. All have, in some way, encapsulated the unique energy of the "target" but none can use the sun-water method as originated.

The first group of essences that we heard about using one of these new methods was a collection of Amazonian orchids. When you are dealing with rare or endangered species it might be felt that collecting a bowl full of blooms would be an environmentally unsound practice. And, considering the flowers might appear several hundred feet up in the tree canopy, dotted here and there throughout the rainforest, this would also be a logistic nightmare to undertake. The solution in this instance was to employ the energies of a quartz crystal as an intermediary, where the perfect lattice structure of the quartz surrogates for the flexible lattice of water, and in some way, receives the energy signature of the plant for a later transference back into water.

Since that time we have come across and used many different methods of essence making. The flower or flowers can be left unpicked and simply bent gently down until they contact the surface of the water in the bowl. Or, more cunningly, a container can be attached to the plant where, for a short period of time, flowers can be held in water. Very recently I saw an ingenious and elegant alchemical device that carefully held the flower in a sealed chamber whilst spring water dripped over it and was collected in a lower chamber. Instead of a bowl of glass some essence makers use beautiful hollow geodes of crystal. Quartz being an extremely sensitive material, it reacts very strongly to intention and so can focus the correct or appropriate energy very accurately into the water. One of the most powerful essences we have ever tried was made by simply placing a clear quartz crystal close to a group of Monterey Cypresses on the California coastline. The essence maker had intended to put the crystal in a fork of the tree but was firmly persuaded by the tree itself to simply rest the stone at the base of its trunk. The crystal was then placed in water and the energy pattern transferred to the liquid. It is also possible to make an essence without any process or intervention at all, except for the focused intention of the maker and the willing co-operation of the plant spirit in question. A sealed bottle already prepared with brandy and water can be left in, or close to, the plant for a specific length of time and the spirit itself infuses or imprints the water. The less human-centred the essence is, the more attention will need to be given to the exact requirements of the "target" plant as to whether crystal, crystal and water, open water, sealed water, sealed water with brandy, pure brandy and so on, it is best to use. Also what time of exposure will be needed; at what time of day; the exact placement of the vessel and the sort of vessel to be used.

All in all, it is probably better to go with the technique that feels most comfortable. This will be the one that creates the least turbulence at subtle levels and so will tend to allow the making of a purer essence. Some essence makers enjoy picking the flowers by hand, feeling that it thus becomes a powerful shared process between human and plant kingdoms, whilst others prefer to leave the plants as untouched as possible. Depending on one's viewpoint of humanity's role and place on the planet, these viewpoints might seem either exploitative or apologetic.

Using Essences

So once we have an essence what can be done with it? How can it be used? Flower essences today are used almost exclusively in the area of healing and the various paradigms of flower essence therapy reflect and expand upon the original vision of Dr Bach. His selection of plant essences addressed what he considered to be the underlying negative emotional states that allowed disease to manifest in the physical body. By some means the energy pattern of each flower encouraged the negative state to transform to its more life-supporting and positive opposite. This view has been generally agreed and expanded upon by all recent essence makers. The specific and unique energy signature of each essence, when introduced in some way into the human auric field seems to enable positive change to come about more easily. An essence acts like a key that can unlock doors that have been shut or blocked. This is an important concept. Many believe that flower essences do not create change by themselves, but they do allow change to take place. This can be compared by analogy to a physical herbal or pharmaceutical preparation that, instead of unlocking the door leaving you free to open it or not, will carry out a full FBI raid with tanks, helicopters, hand-grenades, howitzers and CS gas blowing away anything that comes into their path be it door, wall, hostage-taker or hostage. In some situations such action is necessary, but in the main it can be avoided by carefully stimulating the body's own healing processes. This is the only thing that can heal us, and flower essences seem to be very good at doing this.

Flower essences do not work by belief or faith, nor "placebo effect", because essences work extremely well on animals, small children and plants. However, their actions can sometimes be blocked by negative attitudes or environment factors. Always when working with essences (for whatever reason, healing or otherwise), willing participation and a neutral curiosity are good attitudes to have. It is a good practice to use the essences in a conscious manner.

Focus for a moment on the reason you are taking the essence, whether for healing or whatever. Give the bottle a brief shake before opening. This helps to activate and energise the properties. Visualise or otherwise acknowledge the plant's source, the spirit of the essence. Sit quietly for a moment or two as you absorb the vibrational energies into your system. Don't expect the essence to create mind-blowing altered states, instant healing, revelatory visions etc. every time you use it. All these can happen, occasionally. More often the essences will work at much more subtle levels, creating or allowing energy changes that may take weeks or months to become noticeable.

This is particularly likely when you are in a state of considerable imbalance as with manifest physical illness.

Using a tree essence as a Tree Teacher Technique (see Volume One), the attention will already naturally be focused on a change of perception and will be looking out for subtle differences of feel. Using tree essences as a specific healing technique will be explored further in a later chapter.

How to Use Essences

The classic way of using flower essences is to take three or four drops, three times a day either placed under the tongue and held in the mouth for a little while, or placed in some water and sipped as necessary. No method is better than any other in a general way -as long as the essence comes in contact with the energy field, interaction will take place. Some people will find that certain ways of introducing the essences will work faster or more effectively for them, but it is very much down to personal predilection.

The advantage and disadvantage with the "taking by mouth" method is that it reinforces the comparison with taking medicine, with all the expectations and limitations that comes with such a view. Many people will not feel they have "done it properly" unless they stick to the old, familiar procedures. This is fine. The main disadvantage with the oral taking of essences is one of association rather than effect: it emphasises the "just-another-thing-to-make-me-better" syndrome, and this really is quite a negative, disempowering attitude, reinforcing as it does, the idea that effective healing can only come from outside oneself. It limits the use of flower essences to the role of spiritual aspirin where the name of the essence- the actual plant, gemstone or whatever-is regarded as little more than an identifying label. The stuff in the bottle becomes conceptually isolated from its real source, the plant energy, the living stuff. In this process there is the danger of becoming one-sided, of becoming a spiritual colonialist, simply taking over another part of the world and exploiting it in order to make ourselves "better" without considering reciprocity.

Originally, where taking essences by mouth was inadvisable because of unconsciousness or physical trauma, it was usually suggested that they could be applied topically to the forehead or to the wrist pulses. In fact this proves to be equally effective in most situations. The pulse points of the wrists and the neck and forehead, particularly the frontal eminences, (slight raised bumps on the outer edge of the forehead), are very sensitive to a change of energy and seem a natural place to rub a few drops of essence. You can even pretend it's a perfume or aftershave if you're in hostile territory.

Anywhere where there is a mirroring of the whole systems of the body in a small area is a good place to put the essence. Thus the soles of the feet, the palms of the hands, the ears will all tend to activate effectively.

If you are aware of your own strengths and weaknesses as far as the chakra system is concerned then putting a drop of essence on these points will act as a rapid enhancer and diffuser through that system of interlinked energies. It can often be quite easy to determine our significant points: very often they are those areas that we use a lot and where we tend to get minor health problems. Where we focus our energies is where we can be vulnerable to disorders simply because depletion can more easily occur there. Thus a communicator may be prone to sore throats, thyroid imbalance or neck problems. Someone who works with the heart chakra will be very sensitive to other people's emotions and may have vague heart and lung aches from time to time. A strong solar plexus energy may be prone to food sensitivities, stomach aches and so on.

Because the seven main chakra points are, in effect, gateways or regulators of our energy systems, they are, in any case, important sites for essences. A drop of the right essence on the right chakra can create profound rebalancing that may otherwise take months to accomplish by other means.

The chakra system has the advantage of being fairly easy to comprehend in broad terms and easy to locate on the physical body. Some essence makers who are familiar with the meridian systems of the body have done some exciting work isolating specific meridian points as sites to apply essences for particular results. The meridian system is not easy to master quickly. Unless you have an in-depth knowledge or an accurate testing procedure that you can wholly rely on, plopping essences on acupoints may have an unsettling or even unbalancing effect on the system as a whole. However, if this method appeals to you, consider working with the end-points of each meridian (usually on the hands, feet and head), which will give a general activation to the whole of that meridian.

Aura Sweep

A similar, less structured approach can also be used to introduce the tree essence into the energy field. Called the aura sweep, this is simply rubbing the essence into the palms of the hands and then sweeping the hands around the body through the auric field. The movements can take whatever form is comfortable, but it is a good idea to surround the head, heart and solar plexus as well as paying attention to the arms, legs and soles of the feet. Visualising the essence surrounding the body completely helps to avoid the conceptual "gaps" in the sweep. As the subtle body energies are in a dynamic flow and interaction at all times the essence signature will soon diffuse throughout the auric field. As a final part of this technique, or as an absorption method by itself, bring both the hands, cupped, to the face and breathe deeply-as if you were smelling or inhaling a wonderful scent. Despite there being no scent present this seems to help to bring the essence "inside".

Essence Inhalation

Taste and smell are the most primal of the senses, those closest to identification of physical, molecular matter and so the act of conscious inhalation is psychologically similar to eating. Smelling and tasting is the precursor to ingestion. It is the identification process that allows us to recognise a thing as food or not-food. In some instinctive way inhaling an essence seems more of a commitment than putting a few drops in the mouth - we are taking the energy signature deep inside ourselves where we draw our life from the outside air. With our mouths we can spit out what we dislike, once we inhale deeply we are committed to absorbing the energy carried in the air. The act of raising our cupped hands and breathing deeply is more removed from everyday actions and so more easily slips into a ritual framework. Try it and see how you feel.

Bathing

Even more surreptitious or casual is placing a few drops of essence in bathwater. This will work more effectively if you lay off the bubble-bath, soap, essential oils and rubber ducks and treat it as simply immersion in the essence vibration. Just soak and absorb the essence for a few moments before you start washing. Or better still,(though some might find this excessive), have a bath and wash first and then have a second bath with freshly drawn water to which the essence can be added.

Spraying Essences

Finally, the method we use most often in workshop and lecture situations and which we find works very quickly and effectively in all sorts of environments: spraying the essence using a diffuser sprayer. Large sprayers can be found in garden suppliers, smaller sprays can often be found in cosmetic or bathing sections of chemist shops.

Simply put enough water in the sprayer for your needs and add a couple of drops of the tree essence. Then, remembering to adjust the nozzle to fine mist, spray the essence into the room or around yourself. Because it is such a broad, quick procedure the change in energy feel is usually very noticeable. There will, of course, be a cooling, freshening effect of the atomised droplets, but this cannot account for the rapid change of emotional mood or sense of space when different essences are sprayed around. This process can be likened to stepping into a grove of trees - one is immediately surrounded and immersed in the qualities of that tree. It feels more of an external reality, the air takes on the tangibility of a different environment, and so it often becomes easier for people to recognise and accept a change of internal perceptions and emotions. Again, this is the old programming of accepting "outside" perceptions as "only imagination".

The Chakras

The chakra system has become one of the better known models for working with human subtle anatomies, both in healing and spiritual development. The system first became known to the West through 19th and 20th century translations of Indian treatises, especially from the Tantric schools of Northern India. These texts described seven main wheels of energy (cakra= wheel) aligned along the spine and appearing as spinning vortices of energy. Each chakra was related to specific colours, sounds, deities,qualities of experience, behaviour patterns and overall states of health.

Each chakra is multidimensional, not limited to traditional views and senses attributed to it and each can be viewed as a world in its own right - a living being on another scale. As such it can be imprudent to wish to change the state of a chakra to one that an individual may perceive as being more "evolved".

As we cannot ever be consciously aware of what is going on at every level of each chakra's functioning it is important when working with these energies to set the parameters for our goals in terms of the overall balance and stability of the system as a whole. Otherwise we may find we have an enlightened head in a completely blown out and fused body, for example.

The chakras transmit the life-force into the body, not only from our immediate environment but also from the soul, the complete spiritual essence of who we are. Through these dynamic centres, energy is distributed into the rest of the energy system via the subtle channels or nerves known as "nadis".

The seven main chakras are related physically to major endocrine glands and ganglia of nerve and lymphatic tissue that in some way echo the state of the chakra's energy. Malfunction or disease in a particular part of the body can be related back to the nearest chakras but it is important to remember that the chakra system is completely integrated and finely balanced and if there is imbalance in one area there is going to be a corresponding imbalance in other areas as well.

There is a very common and dubious belief that the "lower" chakras (i.e. those below the heart) are somewhat dirty and smutty, dealing with things like the gross physical world, power and sex. Happiness and enlightenment cannot be gained by ignoring the physical reality of here and now. If we weren't to work with the dust and dirt we wouldn't need to be here on this world at all. If we fail to address the transformation and growth of ALL aspects of our reality then we will not get anywhere, except in a self-deluded mess.

There is also the common misconception of "opening" and "closing" chakras. Firstly if a chakra is closed completely you will find yourself without a body to live in (!) and if you open wide a chakra you may well blow more fuses than you can fix or attract some energy-hungry being (physical or otherwise) who will play havoc with your life and enjoy every moment of your discomfort. The term "shutting down" a chakra is usually meant to signify: returning to normal parameters of function, or sometimes, protecting the energy field from unwanted attention.

Within the boundaries of normal functioning some chakras will be more active than others and when working with energies, meditation or ritual, it is advisable to consciously WILL the chakras to return to everyday balance before resuming normal activities.

Base Chakra

The Base Chakra is located at the base of the spine. In Sanskrit it is known as "Muladhara", which means "root" or "support".

The Base Chakra is vital to the functioning of the individual on every level. It is the foundation upon which all the other energy centres rely for stability and is the major source of useable energy. If the Base Chakra is not functioning well there will be a feeling of unreality, not belonging, not being able to cope, not being able to do anything. Though other chakras might function they will not be able to manifest their reality into the physical world, that is, they will be completely useless. The energy expressed by the Muladhara is solidity, the concretion of form, the experience of existence, the reality of matter and how to use it, the principle of survival.

Second, Sacral Chakra

The Second Chakra, known as the Sacral or Sexual Chakra is called "Svadhisthana" in Sanskrit, meaning "sweetness". It is located in the lower abdomen between the navel and the pubic bone. Whereas the Base Chakra is related to earth and the stillness of solidity, the Sacral Chakra is linked to the movement and flow of energy and the element of water. It is the desire for the Other (the not-Self) which makes the Self reach out and move towards what it desires. This movement is the essential characteristic of all energy and interaction, and the cause of it is desire for pleasure. Once desire and motivation is restricted/suppressed, consciousness has nowhere to flow, creativity dries up, boredom stagnates us and we begin to fear change, the one thing that will stimulate us to a sweeter life. Tension and fear begins to alienate us from ourselves and our environment and energy gets blocked where it doesn't belong, causing illness and disease. Any physical, emotional, mental or spiritual stiffness or constipation suggests you might benefit from work on your Sacral Chakra.

Solar Plexus Chakra

This chakra is called "Manipura" - "lustrous gem". It relates to the element of fire and is concerned with the use of energy and the ability to transform energy into a new level of dynamism within the individual's system. It gives the power to organise and create new states both internally and in the world and as such is related to Power and Will. This centre has so much to do with our relationship to the "outside" world that it can become quite easily exhausted. The Solar Plexus deals on many levels with our ability to recognise and identify the uses of energy from sources other than "us". When it functions well we can easily transform "not self" into "self" to feed our Being. When the Manipura chakra becomes unbalanced we quickly lose sense of direction, lose our ability to deal with life in a spontaneous, creative way. Stress and inhibitions accumulate forcing us either to inaction and apathy or into over-compensating by driving ourselves to workaholic, perfectionist, stomach-melting frenzy. Within the Solar Plexus region is the diaphragm, controlling depth of breathing. The small intestine, stomach and liver all work to transform external matter; identifying what is of use to the body and absorbing it as nutrients. In the same area the spleen plays an important role in the body's immunity - another system that relies on the ability to recognise what is useful and what is harmful to the organism. This chakra also plays an important role in other "self - not-self" barriers, like the skin and nervous system. As a major fuse-box in the body's energy systems it is usually fairly apparent when something blows: immune system compromise, over-acidity, ulcers, digestive problems, malabsorption of nutrients, anxiety and stress, constant colds, insecurity, lack of confidence, hypertension, "burn-out". In fact a great majority of 20th century malaise can be traced to imbalance in the Solar Plexus chakra.

Heart Chakra

The Heart Chakra is "Anahata" - the "unstruck sound" of Creation's vibration. As central point of the chakras, the heart is the integrating and balancing hub of this energy system. When in balance it creates a sense of wholeness and peace, experienced as love. The resonance that is the harmony we feel between ourselves and other people and things is an expression of the Heart Chakra. Where the Solar Plexus absorbs and transforms energy from the environment for the continuation of the Self, the Heart Chakra maintains a dynamic balance between the inner Self and the outer non-Self. We can see this in the function of the organs related to the Heart Chakra: both the heart and the lungs function by alternately expanding and contracting - drawing in and pushing out. Balance and harmony is maintained as long as this pattern of expansion and contraction continues. This equilibrium of opposites is what keeps the flow of life-energy, "prana", moving through the universe.

Throat Chakra

The Throat Chakra is concerned primarily with communication. Communication is the flow of energy from one source to another using symbolic patterns such as speech and image. The Throat Chakra gives us the means to transmit our thoughts, ideas and desires in order to change and maintain our relationship with the world. It only takes a dose of laryngitis for us to discover how fundamental language has become in making ourselves understood and getting cooperation from others!

In many cultures speech, and particularly the naming of things, is seen as a magically powerful act. What can be named can be understood and perhaps then, controlled. This is as true on the subtle, magical levels as it is on the everyday levels. If you do not know the name of an object you want it can be extremely difficult to procure on the physical plane: (a "watchermacallit" or "thingemybob", although expressive is not explicit enough to get you far in a supermarket, for example.) Names of power and names of spirits are powerful because of the accuracy, the resonance, the entrainment, that their spoken sound creates in the universe. Entrainment is when a particular vibration sets up an equal, equivalent vibration in its surroundings. Correctly intoning a name of power, or a mantra, for example, sets up an entrained resonance which, at some level of reality creates the object of invocation itself. Now, the difference between the subtle levels of speech at ordinary levels of speech is the degree of entrainment. In order for a complete energy resonance the name/sound must encapsulate completely and in detail all aspects of that thing - but this sound may not have any obvious meaning in the ordinary levels of thought and speech and has little to do with known language.

The Sanskrit name for the Throat Chakra is "Visuddha" which is translated as "pure" or "purification". This chakra functions by purifying, refining or honing our thoughts and desires to create the maximum degree of entrainment possible, and therefore the best chances of fulfilling our desires. The "purer" the sound of our thoughts, the greater energy they have because the closer they are to the true nature of our desires.

Brow Chakra

The Brow Chakra, also commonly called the Third Eye, is the "Ajna", meaning to know, perceive and command. It is concerned with the understanding and analysis of reality. The Ajna Chakra makes sense of the data received from the physical eyes and the senses. It is also able to go beyond our everyday concepts of time and space to receive images and information from the past and the future (as in memory and in the planning of future events). As our view of reality is an expression of who we are and how we see ourselves in relation to the universe, the Brow Chakra is the centre where our personality is integrated. We usually experience ourselves as being "in" our heads because we are constantly focussed in the Ajna, projecting ourselves into our future - what we reckon will happen next or what we plan to do if such-and-such happens. It is one of the functions of the Brow Chakra to escape from the constraints of time and space in order to gain greater insight.

Danger comes when the chakra loses its balance with the rest of the chakra system and the mind retreats from reality into fantasy and delusion. The depths of this chakra are profound and inviting but without a balanced and equal emphasis on the grounding reality of the Base, Second and Solar Plexus chakras we can float off into the blue with no compass and no anchors, no use to man, beast or spirit.

Crown Chakra

The Crown Chakra is called "Sahasrara" - thousand, referring to the thousand-petalled lotus this chakra is shown as in classical Indian texts. Its location is said to be four finger-breadths above the crown of the head and in some texts is linked to the pineal or the pituitary glands. The Crown Chakra is the organising principal of the chakra system. Within it there is said to exist a replica of all the other chakras and the total pattern of the individual. In this way it is like a projection point from which we are holographically formed. The Crown Chakra is our connection to everything that is. That "everything" is then transformed, filtered and utilised by the rest of the chakra system so that in truth we become a personal lens for the experience of creation by itself. If we remove this link we cannot continue to inhabit a body, but if we foolishly open ourselves to greater voltage than we can use, we can blow a great many fuses and end up no better. Developing our awareness is achieved by tuning into the energy of universal consciousness and bit-by-bit assimilating the new energy levels at a natural, easy rate that the whole of the system is able to adjust to safely. Once these seven main energy centres become habitually balanced and fully functional, other centres and channels will naturally begin to open as consciousness expands.

Using Essences With Chakras

Chakras can be balanced by sweeping an appropriate essence or essences through the aura. Another way of working would be to place or use a particular essence around the area of a specific chakra or chakras. With this last approach it is important to remember that the chakra system is interlinked and interdependent, so using essences in such a focussed way needs extra care.

Subtle Bodies

The chakra system clearly defines different functions and uses of energy in the body. Because of its simplicity and flexibility working with the chakras has become one of the main techniques in healing. What is generally known as the human aura has been identified as a series of interrelated but discrete zones called the subtle bodies. There is less consensus on the exact structure and number of these energy bodies.

Most cultures describe the non-physical bodies in one way or another. Some have two or three, others have five or seven. It can be confusing to try to make sense of different systems, especially as the same names are sometimes used to refer to different things. All systems, be they the chakra, subtle body, meridian or physical are to some extent models and inter-pretations of how things really are. Each system acts as a guide or map to help us but each is on a different scale. So long as we don't try to use more than one map at any one time we shall find our way perfectly well. Mixing scales-using different systems simultaneously-will tend to confuse the outcome. The subtle body system can be thought of as different aspects of the individual as seen from particular perspectives and different vibrational rates. Each layer or level is as much "Us" as our physical self but is not made up of solid matter. In much the same way as a normal photograph shows the external features of a person, an ultra-sound scan shows the internal organs and an x-ray photograph shows only the solid and bony tissues of the body, the subtle bodies represent finer, deeper and more subtle qualities of the self.

Described here is a model of seven subtle bodies, each level extending further from the physical body and constituted of finer energy material. It is important to remember that each

35

succeeding level interpenetrates all the previous levels including the physical, so that there is a continuous, dynamic and complex interaction between them.

The Etheric Body

The etheric body is the closest to the physical, and indeed it is considered to be the energetic blueprint upon which the cells and organs are built. It contains an exact energetic replica of the body with organs and structures the same. When imbalance and weakness occur in the etheric they will eventually manifest on the physical level, so in this respect the etheric body is the last line of defence against disease. Clairvoyant sight describes a blue or blue-grey web of ever-moving energy that extends a little way from the body. The meridian system is believed to be integrated with the etheric body or to act as the interface between etheric and physical.

Giving healing energy to the etheric body will greatly accelerate the repair of physical tissues and may prevent other imbalances from gravitating onto the physical body. The etheric levels are those that often tend to become misaligned from the physical body after shock and trauma. If this mismatch can't correct itself the physical body loses some of its organisational flexibility and this can allow disease states to take hold. Such etheric body dislocation may be the reason why in so many cases a serious period of illness follows a few months after significant shock. Any period of illness or recuperation would benefit from work in this area.

The Emotional Body

The emotional body is the container of feelings. It roughly follows the body's outline but extends further than the etheric. It has no fixed structure and is composed of coloured clouds of energy in continual flux, altering with mood and emotional state. This field is often the aura of colours that sensitives can perceive around a person. The emotional body holds our emotional and psychological stability and our sensitivity to those around us. This body is sometimes called the lower astral, or astral body. This can be confused with the fourth level, here called the astral.

The emotional body is the closest vibratory level to the etheric and contains the volatile and ever-changing energy of our moods. We might think that the environment influences our emotions. Emotion is the weather within us.

For such ephemeral feelings, emotions can play an enormous part in our health and well-being. Each nuance of mood affects the physical body chemistry and even the quality of life-energy that we are able to use. Emotional balance is not an unfeeling, neutral state but a centre point to which the system can return between the extremes of happiness and sorrow. Without this fulcrum/balance/axis as a natural resting place, the emotions can get stuck in a mode of functioning that is inappropriate and deleterious to the body as a whole. Holding on to a particular sort of emotional energy disrupts the whole body weather system.

The Mental Body

The mental body is associated with thoughts and mental processes. It has greater structure than the emotional body and is usually perceived as bright yellow, expanding around the head with mental concentration. Thought patterns exist here as bright shapes coloured with emotion. It is in the mental body that we interpret information according to the belief structures that we have developed since birth.

It has quite distinct and discrete properties. The emotional body reacts, the mental body records, categorises and files these reactions. From birth it constructs how we understand the world and the way it seems to work. It uses all forms of information available to allow the individual to figure out what is going on. The mental body creates our core beliefs and then attaches all other experiences around these central "truths". Unfortunately, the core structures are created very early in life when the tendency is to believe everything we hear and often drastically misinterpret events and the actions of others. Because these structures are so fundamental to our self-image they can be difficult for us to see.

Core beliefs can exist in complete contradiction to each other so that when a certain issue arises in life, the opposite pictures of reality can create enormous stress in the body. This stress very often translates into muscular tension and physical rigidity. Easing mental body issues can allow relaxation at many different levels from posture to tolerance of others' beliefs, to flexibility in problem-solving and finding positive options.

The Astral Body

The astral body is the fourth layer. Resembling the emotional body but with clouds of finer and more subtle colouring, this energy layer contains the essence of our personality. It is the boundary layer between the current individual personality and a more collective spiritual awareness, and is concerned with relationship, particularly the sense of encompassing humanity. It is the container that allows us to recognise ourselves as unique beings located in time and space. The astral body filters and tones down all other sources of energy and information so as not to swamp individual consciousness. It can act as a gateway both into physical manifestation and out towards expanded and collective levels of awareness. Weakness at this level can create great confusion in the perception of reality as the normal constraints of physical reality break down. Too closed an astral body, on the other hand, prevents useful information on other dimensions of energy from integrating into everyday consciousness, which can lead to feelings of unaccountable isolation and loss of direction.

The three remaining subtle bodies are less often described and their functions are not so clearly defined. They certainly are composed of very fine energy. The fifth layer is sometimes called the Causal Body, which links the personality to the collective unconscious and is the doorway to higher levels of consciousness. It patterns the experiences and lessons we have chosen to learn in life. The Causal Body can be seen, by analogy, as the projector that puts our own image onto the screen of physical existence.

The Soul or Celestial Body is the sixth subtle level. It seems to focus fine levels of universal energy and is related to the idea of the "Higher Self".

The Spiritual Body is the seventh subtle body. It is the container and integrator of all other subtle energies. It has access to all universal energies but maintains the individuality of each being. As the finest level that we know of it is all-embracing, encompassing our whole existence in and outside of time and space.

The Meridian System

The meridian system of subtle energy is at the heart of traditional Chinese medicine. Knowledge of the meridians and the acupuncture points located along them requires extensive in-depth study that can take many years. As such, most healers rarely work with this system. There are, however, useful healing procedures that combine the energy of essences with meridian energies in quite straightforward ways. Once there is confidence in an assessment technique, such as dowsing or muscle-testing, the correct choice of a specific essence on a meridian point can make dramatic changes to a person's wellbeing.

The meridian system, as devised by the Chinese, has twelve main energy channels that follow recognised pathways near the surface of the skin. Although it is one integrated system, each meridian has a starting point and an end point, which indicates direction of flow and function. Each meridian is named after an organ or function, such as liver or stomach, but this can be misleading in the West, as the physical organ is only a small aspect of the type of energy a meridian deals with. The functions ascribed to physical organs by the Chinese rarely have any recognisable Western correlations and it is important not to confuse these two very different models of the human body.

It has been generally thought that the meridians are non-physical, or etheric, vessels providing the physical body with the subtle nutrition of Ch'i or life-energy. Recent research suggests that meridians are, at least at some levels, superfine physical structures. The acupuncture points along each meridian often visualised as access points, or energy vortices, like small chakras, have been clearly identified as having a different electrical potential to non-acupuncture points. As well as the twelve meridians that flow on each side of the body, making twenty four channels in all, there are many other vessels that feed the ch'i energy into smaller channels for distribution.

The most important extra channels are the Conception Vessel and Governing Vessel both of which possess acupuncture points and flow up the midline of the body. These two channels help to maintain the flow of ch'i within the entire meridian system and directly affect vitality and health.

The Meridians, Their End-Points and Emotional Connotations

One simple way of understanding some of the functions of the meridians is to associate them with emotional states. Thus a positive emotion will energise or strengthen a meridian, whilst its corresponding negative emotional expression will tend to reduce the energy in the meridian. In this way it is possible to identify some of the underlying emotional energy causing disruption to the system. John Diamond, a pioneering kinesiologist, has discovered the attributions of the meridians and emotional states.

Central Meridian (Conception Vessel)

Begins at the perineum and ends just below the lower lip. Positive emotions are: love, faith, gratitude, trust, courage. Negative states are: hate, envy, fear.

Governing Vessel

Begins at the tail bone, rises up the spine over the head to the centre of the upper lip. There are no specific emotional states listed except as for the central meridian.

Gall Bladder Meridian

Begins at the outer edge of the eye and finishes at the outer end of the fourth toe. Positive emotions are reaching out with love and forgiveness, and adoration. Negative emotions are rage, fury and wrath.

Liver Meridian

Starts at the outside of the big toe and ends just above the bottom of the ribcage either side of the sternum. Positive emotions are happiness and cheerfulness, the negative emotion is unhappiness.

Bladder Meridian

Begins at the inner canthus of the eye (against the bridge of the nose), and ends on the outer edge of the little toe. Positive emotions are peace and harmony. Negative emotions are restlessness, impatience and frustration.

Kidney Meridian

Begins at the ball of the foot and ends where the collar and breast-bones meet. Positive states relate to sexual assuredness, negative states to sexual indecision.

Large Intestine (Colon) Meridian

Begins on the face by the outer edge of the nostril and ends on the inner end of the index finger. Positive emotions are self-worth, acceptance. The negative state is guilt.

Lung Meridian

Begins just below the coracoid process on the shoulder and ends on the inner end of the thumb. Positive emotions are humility, tolerance and modesty. Negative states are disdain, contempt and prejudice.

Stomach Meridian

Begins below the eye at the inner edge of the orbit, and finishes at the outer end of the second toe. Positive emotions are contentment and tranquillity. Negative states are disappointment, disgust, bitterness, greed, nausea, hunger, emptiness.

Spleen Meridian

Begins at the inner edge of the big toe and ends at the side of the chest just below nipple level. Positive emotions are faith and confidence about the future and security. Negative emotions are realistic anxieties about the future.

Circulation-Sex Meridian
(Pericardium, Heart Protector)

Begins at the outer edge of the nipple and finishes at the inside end of the middle finger. Positive states are relaxation, generosity, renouncing the past, letting go. Negative states are regret, remorse, jealousy, sexual tension, stubbornness.

Triple Warmer Meridian (Triple Heater)

Begins at the outside end of the ring finger (third) and ends at the outer edge of the eyebrow. Positive emotions are elation, hope, lightness, buoyancy. Negative states are loneliness, despondency, grief, hopelessness, despair and depression.

Heart Meridian

Begins at the forward edge of the armpit and ends on the inner edge of the little finger. Positive emotions are love and forgiveness. Negative emotion is anger.

Small Intestine Meridian

Begins at the outer end of the little fingertip and ends at the start of the upper edge of the ear in a small hollow of the cheek. The positive state is joy, the negative states are sadness and sorrow.

Meridian Massage

Meridian massage is a quick means to bring an overall balance back to the body. It can be used with another person or by oneself. It can quickly restore energy levels and can reduce a range of symptoms, both emotional, mental and physical.

Procedure to massage another person:

1) Ask the person to stand comfortably with legs slightly apart and arms held away from the body, palms down towards the body.
2) Place a few drops of the appropriate essence(s) on your hand.
3) Begin with both hands over the heart area. Keep an inch or two away from the body throughout.
4) Sweep up to the armpits and along the insides of the arms to the hands.
5) Pass over the fingers and return up the outsides of the arms to the shoulders, meeting again at the throat.
6) Sweep both hands up the face and over the head, following as closely as possible down the midline of the back and then down the outside of the legs to the feet.
7) Pass around the toes and up the inside of the legs and then on up the midline of the torso to the heart. This is

one circuit. The number of circuits and the speed you move is up to you.

8) Complete the process by simultaneously passing both hands up the front and back midlines from base to upper and lower lips. Repeat several times.

If you are massaging another person you will be standing to the front of them. Depending on size you might not be able to fully reach around their back. This is not too important - anywhere where you have to leave the exact line simply use the intention of your mind to complete the sweep across the appropriate area.

Essences and the Meridian System

If there is a general need to strengthen the meridian system it is better to use the techniques such as "meridian massage". A balanced meridian system usually means that, taken overall, there is not a lack of energy or an excess of energy in the system. Individual meridians, or parts of meridians, may be working outside of their normal ranges but in a balanced system a general equilibrium to kept by an excess in one area being balanced by a lack in another. Like every other subtle system, and even the physical systems of the body, a small change in one area may create a larger effect overall. It is not possible to isolate a part from the whole. This means that care must always be taken to carry out only appropriate healing work.

Here is a procedure for working with essences on a particular meridian:

1) Use an arc or list to dowse or muscle-test which meridians need balancing. Remember that, apart from the Central and Governing Vessel, all meridians are in pairs. Determine which side of the meridian pair needs balancing or if both sides require attention.

2) An effective demonstration of an unbalanced meridian can be to lightly touch one end-point with a couple of fingers. If that half of the meridian is out of balance a previously strong muscle-test will go weak. Muscle-testing all meridians in this way, called "therapy localising", will quickly show where work is needed. By "therapy localising" again using the essences, you will be able to check on the efficacy of the rebalancing.

3) In this method it is not important which end-point is touched, so chose whichever is most convenient. The point can be held by either the tester or the patient, if that is easier.

4) Once all twelve meridians have been tested, as well as the Central and Governing Vessels, find which essences will rebalance meridians. If you are dowsing, then work by categories or lists. If you are muscle-testing start in the same way with categories. Once the essence is identified ask which end-point it needs to be placed on. Check to see if essences are needed at one end only or both ends of the meridian, and if the latter, whether different essences are needed.

5) Once the process is completed, recheck all the meridians again to make sure everything is in balance. If muscle-testing, "therapy localise" each point again.

Using Acupuncture Points

Like testing the system as a whole, each meridian will test as balanced where the total energy of the acupuncture points is a neutral balance. This still means that one or more points along any meridian may be seriously over or under-energised and occasionally it is necessary and appropriate to work with single points, other than the end-points. This is usually very powerful and care needs to be taken to ensure that the body has plenty of time to re-adjust and assimilate the changes brought about. It is quite usual for a rest period of several months to be needed, free of any other healing work, to ensure the correction has stabilised.

Procedure:

1) Having determined it is appropriate and safe to work with an acupuncture point, find out which meridian is involved, either by dowsing or muscle-testing.
2) Find out whether the left or right channels are needing work.
3) Find out the exact spot to place the essence by lightly tracing the path of the meridian with your fingertips until the arm or pendulum indicate the right spot. (It is better to trace the meridian in the direction of the natural flow - so start from the beginning of the meridian and work towards the end, this prevent you inadvertently weakening the meridian by moving against the flow.)
4) Note the correct spot where the essence is needed, an introduce a drop to that point.
5) Monitor carefully how the patient feels during the immediate period of time. Sometimes the correction is at such a deep level that nothing much is experienced immediately, but on the other hand, this technique can initiate some strange subjective feelings and emotions.
6) When complete, retest to check that all is OK. Make sure the patient is fully grounded and suggest they drink a little more water than usual for a few days to help the cleansing process.

It is not necessary to know the exact point required if the meridian is traced. If you have a good diagram of the points, identify the necessary place and then check the exact location on the body - it may differ slightly from the diagram.

Trees For Healing

Plants have always been our primary healers and in disguised, synthesised ways they continue to be so today. Before the days of compartmentalisation of knowledge healers would use the many different aspects of plant energy together, a holistic approach that combined herbal and chemical knowledge, with spiritual and magical working to potentiate, prepare and administer plants for healing. Using trees and tree spirits to bring about healing is of the oldest traditions. This chapter will offer suggestions as to how this can be accomplished today.

A hymn in *Rig Veda*, cognised by the seer Bhishaj the physician, son of Atharvan, is addressed to the medicinal plants:

"I think of the hundred and seven applications of the brown-tinted plants, which are ancient, being generated for the gods before the three ages.

Mothers, a hundred are your applications, a thousandfold is your growth; do you who fulfil a hundred functions make my people free from disease...

The universal all-pervading plants drive out whatever infirmity of body there may be...

Let each of you, plants, go to the other, approach the one to the other; thus being all mutually joined together, attend to this my speech.

Whether bearing fruit or barren, whether flowering or flowerless, may they, the progeny of Brihaspati, liberate us from sin.

May they liberate me from the sin produced by curse, from the sin caused by Varuna, from the fetters of Yama, from all guilt caused by the gods.

The plants, falling from heaven, said, "The man, whom living we pervade, will not perish".

The plants, which have Soma for their king, and are numerous and all-seeing, of them thou art the best; be very beautiful to the affectionate heart.

Plants, which have the Soma for your king, who are scattered over the earth, the offspring of Brihaspati, give vigour to this person.

Let not the digger hurt you, nor them for whom I dig you up; may all my animals be free from disease.

All the plants, together with Soma their king, declare "We save him, o king, to whom the seer administers us.

Thou, Soma, art the best of the plants, to thee trees are prostrate; may he be prostrate to us, who attacks us."

(10.8.7 Rig Veda)

Every aspect of trees can be used in healing. The presence of the tree itself, the wood or other physical fragment, the tree essence, the tree spirit, the associated Tree Teacher techniques. All these means are simply ways to introduce the healing energy from the tree into the individual.

It is reasonable and easy to understand how the multifarious chemical components of trees can alter, for good or ill, the functioning of the body and mind. But how can the non-physical, non-ingested, seemingly magical, certainly non-medical, processes bring about any real, lasting change to health and well-being? Very simply it is a matter of understanding how the lack of health has come about, and what mechanisms are maintaining the lack of health, (as opposed to making a full repair and restoration of harmony).

Essentially, illness is a loss of equilibrium that becomes established in any person who is then unable to acquire enough energy of the sort that will re-establish equilibrium. Healing introduces the required energy, or allows the body itself to create the required energy. In traditional societies this imbalance is thought to have come about through wrong action of some kind - the breaking of a taboo, the stepping on the toes of a powerful spirit or god, and so on. These acts disrupt the harmony of the individual within the world and the job of the healer is to mend those bridges and suggest ways the suffering person can placate the spirits. Separation is thus the initiating cause of illness and disease - separation from the sources of sustaining energy, separation from right action. Separation seems to be a particularly human bane, largely born of conscious, thinking awareness and the strong sense of individuality that it creates. Where there is subject and object, "I" and "other", it is easy to acquire the perception of separateness: of discrete, independent, self-sufficient, (and ultimately self-deficient), beings that move upon the world but forget that they are intimately within the world. As one strand of a spider's web is attached and affected by the movement of all the others, so is each life.

Trees are able to exist because they are able to balance all qualities and all elements in their surroundings. Trees are not only in a continual harmonious interacting relationship with their immediate surroundings, they are also by their very nature connected unobstructively with every aspect of universal being. As each species of tree funnels or channels this universal existence in a slightly modified fashion, so the tree makes available a particular quality or expression of wholeness. The underlying, fundamental energy of a tree is the same as every other being within creation - the creative Void, pure awareness, the Absolute. However, the tree, because of its longevity, stability and immobility, is less likely to "forget" that its own apparent self is simply a playful expression of the Void. Unlike human beings, a tree won't get distracted by running around after sense experiences, desires and illusory futures. A tree is in full presence of awareness as itself, is aware of the true emptiness (and fullness), of its nature and is never separated from its source of manifestation. A tree's spirit is the nutritious link between its physical form and non-referential, simple, universal being.

Bringing this memory or experience of unrestricted, complete, comfortable, secure, supportive, non-judgemental, boundless energy into the field of an individual who feels isolated, confused, lonely, in pain, or fearful can help to re-establish that link. It can help to remove that sense of separation within which the illness can maintain its damaging presence. Once the need for a harmonious re-integration has been recognised and accepted, the healing will have begun. The job of the healer is to find the most effective means to bring about this change of heart.

Pathways of Acquiescence

In order for a true healing to occur it is necessary to find the correct energetic pathways whereby the healer and the person receiving the healing agree to the energy outcome - the end result. There must be a coincidence, a synchronisation, or a lining up of energy pathways. Otherwise healing may occur but then regress back to the original unbalanced state, or will not occur at all, or will only succeed in small, minor ways.

What the intention is, what a magician would call "Will", is all-important. Participants need to feel the appropriateness of the techniques used in their healing. To help to understand why this is so necessary consider the following. See each individual as simply a localised folding of a universal, all-pervading energy field - a very small ruck in the tablecloth of existence. This "folding" has boundaries and individual characteristics yet it is still congruent and continuous with the universal field. If this is an accurate view of how things are (and modern physics theory suggests that it is), then all possible energy combinations are always available to the individual.

The only prevention of this flow will be from within the personality or individuality of the "folded" being. Every individual thing, as it becomes more complex, establishes within itself more of a sense of a localised "self": what I am, what I am not, I believe this is so, this is impossible, this is me, this is not real etc. Definition is by its very nature limiting, because it defines negatives as well as positives, thus cutting down on other possible reality scenarios. To give a very simple example, if you believe that you are not the sort of person that visits sex shops it is unlikely you will ever experience that particular bit of reality. A moral idea or belief has limited your knowledge of the world.

An effective healer is one who has these energy pathways unblocked. This doesn't imply that they will be "perfect" in any other respect - simply that their internal constraints allow this sort of flow in healing energy and allows its effectiveness and therefore its success. These are the pathways of acquiescence. The healer must have the constructs (belief systems, energy flows, channels), free that allow a certain process, technique or method to work effectively. This equates emotionally with confidence, the "feel" for it, and being comfortable with the process. The healing must take place on a being who is also allowing the real possibility of change and the movement of energy. The energy pathways between the two must be aligned. There must be no blocks in the pathways of acquiescence.

All traditional healing methodologies accept this need. Hence the use of trance techniques, ritual, formalised behaviour, "sleight of hand", and so on. Each of these activities help to remove barriers to belief, remove barriers to new possibilities and remove the barriers to acquiescence. They encourage the patient to go along with the procedures whole-heartedly. This is neither deceit, nor that muddle headed bluster the orthodox profession trundles out as the "placebo effect". The "placebo effect" is all there is! No amount of intervention and care will bring healing to a person who sees no reason to change from a state of illness to health. Healing can only occur once the pathways of acquiescence have been cleared, not just from one level (such as a superficial "wanting to be better"), but from every level of personal energy, from every underlying cause of limitation, separation, guilt, shock or whatever.

In practical terms, therefore, effective healing techniques need to be found in which you feel completely happy and comfortable with the process and the mechanics. Once there are no blocks, the "Will" or "intention", which is, in truth, focussed and directed energy, will follow thought and healing will flow through your actions.

Healing the whole or healing the bits

When people become ill what they notice are the symptoms - the aches and pains and the way that the body isn't working the way it should. Naturally the main concern is to remove these problems and return to normal as quickly as possible. Symptoms, however serious they may appear in themselves, are simply the apparent manifestation of underlying imbalances. If the symptoms only are dealt with in a healing it would be rather like taking the tip off an iceberg. Remove the tip and the iceberg doesn't disappear, simply another part of it will float to the surface somewhere else. Symptoms are a reflection on the physical level of disturbances on subtle, more powerful and energetic levels of being. Only addressing the symptoms can be rather like looking at yourself in the mirror, seeing a spot, and covering it over by putting a plaster on your reflection to hide it. On one level it seems to have worked, but nothing has been solved.

At practical levels the healer must balance the work so that it can reduce the aggravation of the symptoms whilst getting to grips with the underlying causes of imbalance. This is often a difficult juggling act especially if the only tools available are intellect and the rational deductions of the conscious mind.

Using trees and tree spirits for healing can be a powerful way to re-establish a nutritious, supportive wholeness within which the individual's own energy systems, physical and subtle, can be replenished and strengthened to repair themselves and find a new balance. The way some trees reflect universal energies means that they will be more suited to certain states and conditions of disease than others. However it is important to remember that the identical symptoms in two people may have resulted from completely different underlying causes that have simply created a weakness in the same physical area, thus allowing stress and disease to manifest there. Each individual needs to be seen as a unique aspect of Wholeness, regardless of what is "wrong". The aim is to bring more light into the dark room rather than analyse and map the exact qualities of the darkness.

The process of healing is purely a self-initiated process. The healer is simply someone who helps, not someone who heals. Each person is wholly responsible for their own life. This is not a moral judgement, but the true nature of things. The effective healer offers situations and energy patterns which increase healing support and self-repair. When working with tree energies the healer is simply the mediator who introduces those trees to the ill person and monitors the resultant changes.

Illness creates fear and confusion. In these states it often becomes impossible to view things from a balanced and sensible perspective. At these times we all need someone else to give us advice and support. Although the healing motivation comes wholly from within, compassion and caring wisdom are the characteristics of the Absolute, the wholeness of things, and are the only things that will counteract isolation and separation - the ultimate cause of all disease. Through the compassionate concern of the healer the far greater compassionate wisdom of the trees can be brought into the energy field of that person. There are many ways in which this can be done.

In the Presence of Trees
There is little that can better the experience of being within the energy field of trees themselves. All the senses are energised and flooded by the presence. The mind and the emotions are profoundly altered, and rapid re-integration of energy can occur. No formal ritual practices or healing processes are necessary in such circumstances. It is simply a matter of offering oneself and asking for support and healing. There need be no prescription nor any instructions - the heart should be the guide and the mind should be receptive and listening. Unfortunately few people these days would feel comfortable with such simplicity. Only a few would really accept that finding a tree that draws the attention and which is restful to be near, then asking for a sharing of energy and healing, could really solve seemingly intractable problems. Some people might like a slightly more formalised approach, in which case an exercise like centre-line breathing or the following procedure from Chi Kung can be suggested.

Standing Like a Tree
Zhan Zhuang (J'an Jong) means "standing like a tree". It is a system within Chi Kung that focuses on powerful, stationary, standing poses. Two exercises offer ways to experience and unite with the energies of a tree.

The first begins by standing near a large tree; allow your system to calm and become relaxed. Stand easily with feet about shoulder width apart, knees slightly bent, belly relaxed.

Imagine that your whole body is suspended from the top of your head. Your weight is evenly balanced in the centre of your feet, your arms and hands are gently relaxed.

Now allow the tree to become your sole object of focus. Imagine a circuit of energy extending from the crown of the tree down to the top of your head. This energy flows through you and out of the soles of your feet back down to the roots of the tree.

This creates a cycle of natural energy flowing through both yourself and the tree. Your energy field becomes a part of the tree within one circuit - the essentially identical harmonious core power that is both yourself and the tree. As the tree's energy flows into your head from above, breathe it in and consciously draw the energy deeply into yourself. If there is an area of imbalance or illness of which you are aware then allow the energy to bathe that area. As you breathe out, the energy will flow out of your feet into the ground and will once again rejoin the tree at its roots.

There should be no worry or fear of negativity affecting the tree. Illness is simply energy in the wrong place at the wrong time, there is no sense of "passing on" the disease or disturbance. Illness has come from some separation from creation. As the tree is continually connected to creation it cannot be brought into disharmony this way. Also, you have been drawn to the tree in the first place, so there is a heart connection there and a willingness to offer healing energy. Your energy will also infuse the tree with your unique humanity and your appreciation and sharing are positive, nutritious elements.

The second exercise opens a circuit of energy in a different direction.

Stand facing a mature, strong tree and begin by adopting the initial standing pose: feet balanced and placed firmly shoulder-width apart, relaxed arms and belly, head as though linked to a suspending line.

Open your hands outwards, palms facing each other as if embracing the air in front of you. Point the fingers of both hands gently towards the tree.

Imagine a circuit of energy that passes from the tree to your left hand as you breathe in.

As you breathe out, the energy passes through your right fingertips and circles back to the tree.

Continue with this process until you feel it is time to stop.

Remember that, generally speaking, the larger and more mature the tree, the stronger the healing potential.

The same basic exercise can be adopted for working with a group of trees or within a wood. Allow variations to develop according to the surroundings that you are in.

Don't forget your "please" and "thank you's".

Energy Signatures

Where it is not possible to work with the trees themselves, or in addition to this, there are methods that employ the energy signatures of the trees. Whatever is a carrier of the signature will automatically introduce that tree's vibration into the auric field. Whether a tree essence, or a piece of wood, it will act as a key that opens the door to that tree spirit's characteristic energy. The human subtle energy system is a complex, interpenetrating web of forces in dynamic equilibrium. Bringing another energy field like that of a tree essence, will immediately bring about changes in that field - no matter where it is placed. There are, however, certain areas of the body that will be more sensitive and more efficient, or simply more relevant to the nature of the disease.

There can really be no hard and fast rules about such placements - the interactions of healer and patient at a particular time and place will always be unique. If you have a testing technique such as pendulum dowsing or muscle-testing these can be used to find the most appropriate locations. Simply allowing your body intelligence or intuition to identify by "feel" where the tree energies are most required is a good way to work. If you don't trust your own senses you are either not grounded and centred enough or you have a lack of trust - in which case time needs to be spent re-examining why you are wanting to work in this way. Remember that it is not you doing the healing. Your wish is to help by introducing holistic tree energy. Let that tree energy take over the healing process. Avoid expectations of success or failure. Simply be attentive and open to what is happening.

Small pieces of wood from a whole variety of trees can be used in a healing. They can be selected and placed on and around the body. At each placement allow a moment to settle the energy, then ask if any sensations or changes can be felt. In our experience such placements of simple bits of wood can be as transforming an experience as using crystals and gemstones.

Shaped sticks or simple wands can be used for directing energy into areas needing healing or can be used to draw out blocked or stagnant energy. Use the direction of the mind with focused intention to create the most appropriate flow.

The seven main chakra points are useful locations, and a familiarity with the basics of the chakra system can be a good start for accessing subtle energy patterns. Pulse points, such as at the wrists, the temples and the sides of the neck will absorb the tree energies rapidly. There are also reflex points on the hands and feet that correspond to all the parts and organs of the body. Working on these areas can be a simple and powerful way to assess and correct imbalances.

The bone in the back of the hand that runs from the first finger joint back to the wrist bones at the base of the thumb corresponds to the entire spine and its subtle and physical reflex points. Placing tree essences here, or working with woods, will help to correct imbalances in the whole body. Points that are sensitive to light pressure along this bone will indicate areas needing attention. The same process can be carried out on the sides of the feet, from the big toe to ankle, or from little toe to heel.

Symptomatic versus Constitutional

Within homoeopathy it is recognised that everyone has one or two constitutional remedies. These are those that, whatever the nature of the disease or the symptoms, will always tend to improve health and energy levels. These remedies are those that match most closely the natural balanced state of that individual - they reflect the constitution, the way in which the energy tends to be used. Constitutional remedies are thus a sort of homoeopathic "power animal".

We likewise have constitutional affinities to certain trees. One or two trees will most closely match our needs and drives in their own energy makeup, and they will always be a support to us whether we are healthy or otherwise. These trees may not be our "favourites", nor even a tree with which we are familiar, but if there are difficulties in any area of our lives it is worth considering whether a particular tree energy would be helpful to us. As our circumstances continually change, so the tree energies that will bring us most balance will also tend to change. As our essential nature, our unique personality traits, tend to remain the same through all exterior events, so the constitutional tree energy reflects that basic nature and therefore its positive aspects.

Using several tree energies together can greatly speed up the healing process. The constitutional energy will reinforce our core life-energy levels whilst one or more other trees might address the precise health problems that we are experiencing. Where the constitutional energy is a really close match it will initiate healing at deep levels by itself. The other energies may simply help to focus more closely on the symptomatic imbalances so that they can be released a little faster.

Plant Spirit Healing

These previously mentioned techniques use some physical thing, an essence, or a piece of wood, or the presence of the tree itself as a way to transfer energy into the healing situation. Correlates of this sort of healing can be found in all traditional contexts but the primary function of these processes is usually to introduce the spirit of the plant or other healing substance into the patient so that it can do the work. Plant spirit medicine, as this type of healing has come to be called, has many advantages. Firstly the healer is in no doubt who is doing the healing: it is the spirit that will cure or not cure the disease. The human healer is simply the intermediary, the skilled technician who knows how to ask the right spirits to come and help.

Where there is a link to an especially powerful spirit, the healer may be able to deal with a wider variety of conditions, regardless of symptoms, just with one plant. Even when the spirit itself is unable to work directly on the problem, it can be asked to find the help of another spirit and so work indirectly with the disease. In cases that are difficult to deal with, as for example an illness caused by the negative energies of another powerful person (usually at an unconscious level, and very often another family member), it can be tricky for another human to get involved because the negativity can sometimes turn on the healer's own energy as well. Asking for the spirit itself to deal with it, removes other human involvement and any streams down which the negativity could flow.

Where there is an awareness that the spirits themselves are doing all the hard work there can be an easier relationship between healer and patient. Neither expects it to be someone's "fault" if the healing isn't able to be complete. There is less danger of a complicated ego-involvement that invests too much energy on an outcome prestigious to the healer.

Plant spirit healing is usually no different in appearance to any other kind. Very often the healer is working internally to ask

60

and direct the spirit energies. These can be introduced into the patient by touch, or administering a herb or medicine, an essence, or contact with an object of transferral, be that a crystal, piece of wood, smoke or whatever.

Before spirit healing can be really effective the healer has to have a deep and intimate connection to the spirit or spirits with which she works. This involves much personal exploration of each spirit's capabilities and predilections. Returning to the example of the South American "curanderos", they use the spirit songs they have learnt, the "icaros", to invoke the healing spirits that they have come to know through the years of apprenticeship. During the healing process these invoked spirits allow the "curandero" to heal and other spirits may also appear to offer advice and information useful to the desired outcome.

Using the mantra or chant suggested in the Tree Teacher Techniques would be one way to begin to work with the energies of a particular tree spirit. Once a rapport has been established it is quite likely that a powerful, personal song or chant will be taught by the spirit, either as a variation or expansion of the original sounds, or as a completely new pattern.

No tree can be said to be a better healer or spirit helper than any other. It is a question of working with them until one or two emerge as energies with which you can work confidently within a healing situation. It is most likely that there will be one or two main tree spirits with whom you work, other spirits coming and going in response to the patient's needs.

The Spirit of Cherry

One evening in April attention turned to a young cherry tree that was in full blossom, visible across the valley from our house. Becoming more receptive and open to the unique energy, a waking dream, or vision, of the cherry spirit developed. From the body of the tree emerged a pale whitish form resembling a young woman. As this spirit approached, its energy multiplied and increased in vigour. These outpourings of energy took the form of young children whose nature expressed the healing quality of the tree. Like the petals of cherry blossom these numberless spirits were guided by the intelligence of the spirit awareness from which they had emerged, but their nature was very different. Whilst the female spirit seemed compassionate, the child sparks or petals were sensuous, boisterous, completely uninhibited and joyous. Like small toddlers with unlimited passion and confidence it seemed they would gravitate towards an area of pain and illness - any part of the body for which there was fear or rejection or disgust - and by their simple, sensuous enthusiasm would repair the negativity by unrestricted natural outpourings of life-energy, effectively sweeping away the fractures of separation.

The essence of wild cherry, or gean, can be effective as a smoothing, pain-reducing remedy mainly because it enables a harmonious flow of energies to be re-established. The vision that evening was simply another way in which the tree energy was interpreted into visual form. Being such a vivid experience, and quite unlooked for, the cherry has become an important healing tree, especially where the physical body is under great stress. The spirit of cherry will soften the hard edges of disease and denial and help to allow change and other healing energies to enter. The cherry for others, though, presents a very different imagery and perhaps very different functions. Some have seen cherry as a knight in armour, for example.

We each have our own pathways of strength and weakness, our individual clear energy channels and those that remain blocked. Those trees and spirits that can help the healing of others are those with which we can integrate well and that encourage and amplify our own connection to the healing wholeness which is every being's true nature.

Spirit Medicine

There is a technique within the traditions of Tibetan tantric medicine that can be adjusted slightly to allow the Tree Teacher Techniques to be effectively used as a focused spirit medicine. The Indian and Tibetan healing systems are fundamentally holistic in approach and aim not simply to remove illness, but to remove the causes of illness as well. This perspective encourages a growth of awareness and consciousness so that mistakes both of behaviour and of understanding are less likely to set up the seeds for future problems. Preparing and prescribing medicines are, therefore, accompanied by ritual processes that enhance the life-giving qualities of the herbal and mineral ingredients. The Tibetan physician will repeat the mantra of a specific aspect of the Healing, or Medicine Buddha, most suited to counteract the illness within the patient. Visualising the form of the awareness-being ("yidam", usually loosely translated, rather inaccurately, as "deity"), whilst repeating the mantra, the healer will count out a certain number of repetitions and then blow the accumulated energy into a special container made of yak horn or wood called a "nakru". This horn, like a powder-horn, has a removable stopper, sometimes containing a small spoon, at the wide end so that herbal medicines, either loose or in the form of shaped pills, can be placed within. A small hole in this lid or at the narrow end of the horn is where the mantra and visualised energy can be blown to infuse the material inside.

So having chosen the most appropriate herbal ingredients the healer spends some time in meditation and then begins to use the visualisation and mantra building up the energy and periodically exhaling it into the nakru. At the end of the process there is a powerfully potentised medicine that will help to create positive change at every level of the patient's body, emotions and mind.

Translating this process to work with tree energies a whole range of possibilities presents itself. Firstly, the nakru can be made from a cow horn (yak being more difficult to find!), or can be fashioned from an appropriate wood. A largish branch can be shaped into a horn shape and carefully hollowed out, or the traditional design can be abandoned in favour of a more simple turned pill-box, or even a deep bowl. A sealed vessel of some kind might accumulate the energy better than one that is open, but experimentation with different shapes would be worthwhile. The wood chosen can vary depending on the quality of healing energy required. Energising, protecting woods like yew, willow, bay or olive could be used for stimulating life energy. Black poplar, oak or holly might have a more stabilising and cumulative quality. Cherry, lime, plum and maple would bring a powerful but gentle healing energy, and so on.

Next to consider is the vehicle for the infused tree energy. This too, could be from a tree whose qualities seems sympathetic to the aims. Leaves, bark from twigs, flowers, fruit could all be used - though if they are to be taken internally in some way, as a tea or incense, it is important to be absolutely sure that there is no toxicity. Lime flowers, elder flowers, willow bark, elm bark and others have useful physical herbal properties and make pleasant infusions. If the potentised material is to be used as incense, for example, aromatic woods like juniper, cypress, sandalwood, cedar, or apple could be included. Other pleasant and healing herbs can be considered: mint, thyme, skullcap, dandelion, basil, lemon balm, or a completely neutral substance like the sac-lac tablets used in homoeopathy could be placed into the nakru for energising.

Once these steps have been carried out prepare yourself by sitting quietly, balancing your own energy fields and then attune by whatever methods you find most effective to the energy of the tree you wish to infuse into the medicine. Repeat the tree mantra or chant, either for a certain length of time, say ten or fifteen minutes, or count out a number of repetitions using a string of beads, grains of rice, or pieces of wood.

64

At the end of each cycle blow with force and focus the accumulated tree energy into the nakru. Sit quietly to recollect yourself and then repeat the cycle as many times as you feel appropriate. At least to begin with, only sit for short periods of time. Unless practised the mind will wander after a few minutes and the quality of the energy will begin to weaken. Take several days to build up the accumulated energy within the nakru.

Begin by making up this spirit medicine with yourself and your own needs in mind. It is a powerful method to get to know the qualities of a tree spirit. Take the opportunity both to learn and to create healing within yourself.

In the Tibetan tradition each yidam has a powerfully characteristic form that can be a focus of visualisation for the mind. The speech is occupied with the mantra repetitions and the body is involved with holding the prayer-beads ("tengha"), and counting each repetition.

A picture, photograph, leaf or twig of the tree can be used to hold the attention if you are unable to work within the sight of the tree you are infusing. Also the visual symbol if known or discovered would act as an appropriate focus for the mind. Using the tree essence will also help you to keep attuned to the energy without effort. If there is any discomfort or distraction that prevents the clarity of your intention, simply leave the process until conditions are more suitable.

Asking for Help

Wherever there is doubt about the correct course of action in a healing situation, go directly to the tree teachers and listen to what is offered as a way forward. Even the simplest of suggestions, when carried out to the letter, will sometimes bring amazing results.

Remember that healing doesn't always mean complete cure. Valuable work can be done at emotional and spiritual levels even where the physical body has received so much damage that recovery looks very unlikely. Nothing lives forever, and death cures all diseases. To take away fear and offer support is the compassionate action of a true healer, a very tree-like quality of stillness and support.

Healing Trees

Using this section

We all have the understandable desire to want to know once and for all "what-does- what", with no doubts, no equivocation, no alternative possibilities. Unfortunately this is not a particularly realistic wish and more importantly, it tends to foster an unhealthy reliance on "experts' advice" at the expense of real personal knowledge.

We would like to re-emphasise that the information presented here is, at best, a partial map of the energy landscape of each tree. If one is drawn to a certain tree to restore a health imbalance, don't reject that feeling simply because the description here doesn't seem to mit. You and your body are usually the "experts" when it comes to understanding at deep levels the underlying causes and scenarios of your own energy situation.

Each tree will tend to foster a tendency towards integrating wholeness. Simply, some will do that more speedily and harmoniously than others. Choosing to work with one or two trees doesn't preclude changing to others. Energy is in continual movement and flux. Sometimes a brief interaction with a tree of one species will be all that is required before moving onto others.

With a testing skill such as muscle-testing or pendulum ciowsing, choices can be made with apparent ease and conviction. However, these techniques are simply means to ampiiil, and make apparent, energy information that the body, mind and intuition already possess.

Letting your eyes drift gently across the tree list you will inevitably settle and focus on one or two. Opening the pages "at random" can also reveal some useful and pertinent information. (In fact, rather than ploughing through all the trees in alphabetical order from A-Z, which will inevitably lead to a constipation of details, just now and then, read a page or two.)

If there is a particular circumstance or imbalance wishing to be addressed, simply focus on that for a moment before scanning the text. There are a few pages at the back of the book left for your own notes. Use these pages to collate useful information, for instance, grouping trees that seem to share characteristics or that suit certain individual's energy profiles.

Alder
(Alnus glutinosa)

Key: RELEASE; ANXIETY; TENSION; INCREASED LIFE-ENERGY; WELL-BEING; FLOW; STABILITY; PROTECTION; ORANGE-RED.

Alder grows throughout the British Isles along rivers and streams. The lack of oxygen in the wet soil is no problem to the tree as its roots are home to nitrogen-fixing bacteria that help to free up nutrients the alder can use. In fact the common, or black, alder prefers to have its dark red roots growing in a constant flow of water. These roots are a significant factor in the maintenance of our riverbanks and also increase the fertility of the soil.

In winter alder stands out as a tall wall of upright trunks and purple-black branches scattered with the cone-like black seedcases. In early spring male catkins begin to fill out turning the tree a reddy orange before the deep green glossy leaves show.

Alder when cut turns orange - red, and thus joins yew and blackthorn as a "bleeding tree". The timber is used where constant wetting and drying occurs as it is extremely resistant to rot. As a coppice it provides fast-growing poles for smallwork and high quality charcoal.

Alder essence focuses in the abdominal area where it can strengthen the stomach, liver and gall-bladder. It reduces nervousness and anxiety that arises from known causes and that are consciously disturbing.

The Central meridian (Conception Vessel), which provides a source of primary life-energy to the meridian system and which

69

Alder

focuses on survival issues and self-identity, is energised. Stomach and Small Intestine meridians are also activated promoting an increase of happiness and joy.

A clarity is brought to the mind and the mental body especially associated with thought processes and belief systems. With this cleansing of the mental body related physical tensions can be eased, so that alder is useful for muscular tension that has an emotional component. (Combines well with dandelion extract or essence for relaxation of muscle tissue).

The chakras at the heart and solar plexus are activated. This increases the sense of well-being and life-energy available, which naturally reduces anxiety levels. Energy is able to flow from the solar plexus to the heart across the diaphragm which is often a source of blockage to the flow of energies because of stress and tension accumulated there. When the heart chakra receives more energy the entire system becomes better balanced and is able to release stored stresses more easily. This may be expressed as involuntary deep breaths, sighs or crying.

All these qualities of alder combine to increase the speed of action, effectiveness and absorption of other remedies.

Signature: Root nodules that free trapped nitrogen from waterlogged soil : the essence has the ability to release deep tensions and increase the life-energy available.

Alder exists within the dynamic flowing environment of moving water, yet it stabilises all elements, reintroduces life and remains flexible.

Comments: Traditionally associated with Bran the Blessed, god of the Underworld, a protector and rescuer from death, a friendly giant. Bran is associated with the Celtic cult of the head. The head was seen as a receptacle of power, protection and wisdom. The black seed-capsules of alder look like miniature heads hanging from the purple-black branches of midwinter. Dwelling on the boundary of different worlds - earth and water - alder, with its imperishable wood used by builders, smiths and smelters is a tree of fire, durability and the force of life.

Alder provides many dyes from its parts: bark alone gives red and is the basis for black dyes, bark and young shoots give yellow and shades of orange-pink, fresh wood provides a pinkish fawn, catkins give green.

Alder bark is tonic and astringent, useful for swellings and inflammations, particularly of the throat. Bags of heated leaves are said to cure rheumatism.

Apple
(Malus domesticus, Malus sylvestris)

Key: DETOXIFICATION; BALANCE OF PURPOSE; MOTIVATION; LUST FOR LIFE; SELF-WORTH; THE HEART OF THINGS.

Wild crab apple is native to Britain and found in hedgerows and oakwoods. Wild apple has mainly white flowers and some thorns. It is one of the original species from which the sweeter, larger domestic apples were grown. Domestic apples found in gardens and orchards are also common along paths and roadsides where discarded cores have been thrown. They are thornless and tend to have a larger, more pink tinged flower. Most other decorative crab apples have been introduced from the Far East. Cross-breeding and the many varieties of apple can make exact identification difficult. Domestic apple varieties have downy leaves while wild crab apple's leaves are hairless.

With apple there is an increased balance of purpose, a clarity and ability to express needs precisely. With this influx of discrimination it becomes apparent which aspects of life are not productive, or that are even damaging. Choices can then be made to abandon inappropriate patterns in favour of those that will allow a growth of happiness and fulfilment.

The Large Intestine meridian can be cleansed, particularly of that sort of energy that creates apathy. With increased motivation there can be a greater assimilation of healing energy and repairs can be made to stressed or damaged tissue. The Circulation-Sex meridian (Pericardium, Heart Protector), is also given a boost where introverted cycles of gloom or jealousy are an issue. Here energy is focused on life-supporting, creative goals and the wise use of available resources.

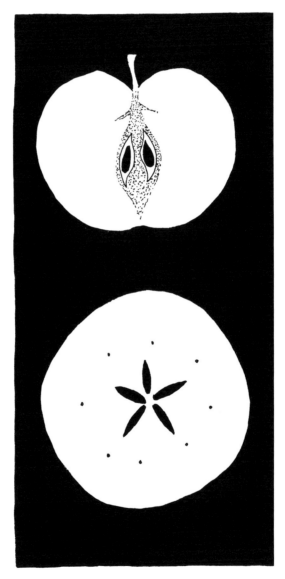

Apple

The heart chakra is greatly affected by apple's energy patterns. A cleansing and balancing of this area helps to give clarity to our spiritual direction and personal path - so apple can be used for indecision or doubt as to actions. There is a greater desire to enjoy life, to learn and make use of experiences. This can help both the timid to explore further and restrain the overly reckless from impulsive action. Perceptive insights become sharper and there is a greater access to higher states of awareness and the information that can flow from these levels.

The emotions are stabilised and directed into constructive channels whilst still maintaining a healthy lust for life. Harmony and understanding others becomes easier. Spiritual nature is opened up to wisdom, healing, a clearer understanding of self and to new areas of perception and inspiration.

In practical terms these effects strengthen the immune system via the thymus gland and speed up the removal of toxins through the large intestine. Clarity of mind and emotions reduces tension, and this new relaxation makes spiritual energies more easily available.

Signature: The cross section of the fruit is heart-shaped. The high roughage content and pectin within the fruit help to cleanse the physical system. The sharp juice of crab apple focuses the attention in the present.

Comment: Apple has been used as an effective detoxifier and cleanser for many years now. It can be a useful adjunct where there are issues of self-worth and feelings of guilt or uncleanliness. Equally apple can help when trying to avoid or give up inappropriate behaviour. Several times tobacco smokers have commented that it helps reduce the need for nicotine, or actually reduces the enjoyment of smoking after taking the apple essence into the auric field.

As a symbol apple has been connected to the sun, the yearly cycle, and the realms of the Otherworlds, particularly of Immortality and the Afterlife in Celtic, Norse and Greek mythologies. The picture can be somewhat clouded as the term "apple" has often been used as a generic term for many different types of fruit.

It is interesting to note that the pattern the planet Venus appears to make around the Earth over a several year period is the shape of an apple's cross section, and that apples are many times linked to goddesses of love and beauty.

Ash
(Fraxinus excelsior)

Key: STRENGTH; HARMONY WITH SURROUNDINGS; STABILITY; SECURITY; FLEXIBILITY; YEAR OF MOONS.

Ash is a native forest tree that can grow to 130 feet. The leaves are long and made up of nine to thirteen stalked leaflets that give the tree a light, graceful appearance. Male and female flowers appear before the leaves on the same or on different trees, springing like a gush of water from just behind the black buds at the branch-tips. Ash is usually one of the last trees to come into leaf and the earliest to drop in autumn.

The wood is strong, white and flexible - it is said to be able to bear more weight than any other wood. Ash bark has been used as a tonic and astringent, the leaves as a laxative.

Ash brings the strength to stand up for yourself in a way that is in tune with your surroundings. An acknowledgement and exploration of personal status that leads to clear understanding of how one interacts with the world and establishing a harmonious relationship.

The Central meridian, running from the perineum up the front of the body to the lower lip, is strengthened. This stabilises personal energies, vitality and integrity. It ensures the rest of the meridian system is energised.

The base chakra and heart chakra are energised, and this in turn strengthens the sense of reality and the ability to cope with the world, and to feel at home with oneself and the life one is leading.

Ash

There is an increase in love and the ability to express feelings in a strong yet compassionate way. There is a steady growth of flexibility and adaptability.

The astral, causal and spiritual subtle bodies are aligned. This balances the Higher Self and its relationship to the collective consciousness of race and planet, encouraging a sense of security and rightness about one's place in the scheme of things.

At a physical level ash helps to strengthen the bones and increases the general flexibility of the physical system.

Signature: Despite its great size ash doesn't block light from other plants.

The timber is flexible and easy to work when first cut, becoming much harder as it dries.

Comment: The fact that ash has a silvery grey bark and leaves with between nine and thirteen segments aligns it to lunar aspects of the goddess. (Nine is the magical three- times- three, sacred to the Celtic peoples and their forerunners; thirteen is the number of full moons in a lunar year.)

Ash is often associated with Norse legends of the World Tree, Yggdrassil, though this has been suggested as a misinterpretation of the name for another tree, the yew. Ash was used for the shafts of spears and also for bowmaking. The former use links it directly to the Ancestor Wisdom god of the Norse peoples, Odin, Woden, Wode, Wade . Yggdrassil means "horse of Ygg", and Ygg is another name for Odin himself. Despite being head of the Aesir Indo-European deities, Odin learnt most of his magical and shamanic powers from earlier cthonic energies like the giants and the goddesses of the Vanir, the older fertility deities of Neolithic times.

Bay

Bay
(Laurus nobilis)

Key: ENERGY; DEEP RED; PROTECTIVE; FIERY; GROUNDING; STIMULATING; KEEPING AT BAY; BLOCK RELEASE; ENERGY BOOST; APOLLO.

Bay, sweet bay or bay laurel, is a native of the Mediterranean area. Usually planted in gardens for its aromatic leaves, bay rarely grows higher than twenty-five feet in Britain though it can grow well over twice this height in warmer climates. The entire tree has a high content of aromatic essential oil - the glossy evergreen leaves and smooth, dark purple-brown twigs burn easily with a heavy scented smoke. It is possible that bay smoke was an ingredient of the incense used by Classical oracles, as it is narcotic and excitant. Internally it is a dangerous oil, increasing blood pressure and heart rate. Externally it can be a useful warming poultice for aches and bruises. From Roman times it has had associations with Apollo and protection from harm, both from disease and spiritual harm. The trees are male or female with yellow flowers clustering at the leaf bases in spring. Female trees produce glossy black berries.

Bay essence has a deep-rooted effect on the whole of the body. It gives an energising boost that some may find too strong for comfort. Bay is a deep red energy, strongly grounding, and this may give rise to explosions of energy as blocks are released. Even as a vibrational essence bay will encourage the blood flow and so it can be useful where there is sluggish energy or poor circulation at the extremities. Those with heart conditions should avoid using bay or use only with extreme caution. (Hawthorn and blackthorn may be safer alternatives).

81

Bay can encourage the expression of suppressed or hidden emotions, particularly strong ones like anger. Combined with apple an effective cleansing of the emotional system can be encouraged.

The tree is very protective. It enhances the entire meridian system and stimulates the physical. At the other end of the spectrum , bay draws down a powerful vortex of spiritual energy through the upper chakras which can remove and neutralise negative thought-forms and other harmful influences.

Signature: The deep, pungent red oil characterises the protective, fiery, and earthily stimulating qualities of this tree.

Comment: The Oracle of Delphi was the primary religious centre of ancient Greece and was under the protection of the Sun God Apollo. Bay laurel was sacred to Apollo.

Working with the wood fills the air with pungent scent. It has a smooth grain and can have an unusual grey-purple tinge.

Bay oil because of its toxicity is not easily available. It does however make an excellent psychic shield. The smallest dab on the finger can be rubbed around doors and window frames to "keep at bay" all sorts of psychic mischief.

Beech
(Fagus sylvaticus)

Key: EASY-GOING; OPENNESS; COMMUNICATIVE; INTERNAL STRUCTURES OF CREATIVITY; HOPE; CONFIDENCE; RELAXATION; ORANGE.

Beech will grow easily on any soil except heavy or clay soils (where oak flourishes), and it will eventually dominate any woodland, particularly on chalk and limestone uplands. Young trees need to be protected by other species until they are established and are able to tolerate exposed conditions.

Beech has a nearly cylindrical trunk that can reach to 100 feet (30 m) over 120 years. When not crowded beech will start branching fairly close to the ground and these low branches have the characteristic of holding their copper coloured leaves throughout the winter months. The bark is thin, smooth and silver-grey - making beech one of the most beautiful and sensuous looking of British trees.

Beech flowers in May and bears fruit, "beech mast", in October. A heavy mast year usually follows a hot summer the previous year. Beech mast is an important food source for many animals and used to provide extra fodder for pigs in autumn.

Beech brings creativity to the highest level of the self. This doesn't necessarily mean any outward form of expression, it is more an internal creativity, a building up of the self within the self - a healing and accepting of one's true nature. This gives confidence and security.

There is a relaxation of the muscular system especially in the areas of the head and solar plexus. These areas are often involved with tension and anxiety headaches.

Beech

Beech increases hopefulness and confidence. It allows one to release and express personal potential more fully. Fears about the future, despair and loneliness are reduced.

Those who lack confidence in speaking, suffer from sore throats, or who have a difficulty in demonstrating their abilities often indicates a block at the throat chakra that beech essence will help to clear.

The emotional body is relaxed where there are difficulties with self-image, particularly in the areas of sexuality and body image. Reproductive problems that arise from emotional tension can be helped. Trauma and shock at the emotional levels can be released, leading to relaxation and a more open, easy-going nature.

At the finer mental levels of the causal body, beech essence brings an easier flow of information and a more harmonious structuring of energy links that results in an increased sense of peacefulness and joy. It also allows a clearer means of expression in a more structured, rational and logical manner.

Signature: Mature beech trees often resemble lithe human forms. The smoothness and the characteristic copper-orange leaves suggest a deep relation with the energies of the sacral chakra: creativity, sensitivity, sensuality, enjoyment of existence.

Comment: Beech tar was used externally for skin diseases and internally for chronic bronchitis. It is stimulating and antiseptic.

Bird Cherry

Bird Cherry
(Prunus padus)

Key: SENSUALITY; BODY RELAXES; TOLERANCE; EMOTIONAL HEALING; FEELING; PLEASURE IN PHYSICAL EXISTENCE; PINK-ORANGE.

The bird cherry is a smaller native cherry than the gean and is more common in the north of Britain. Varieties are widely planted for their spectacular sprays of white flowers that open in May when the gean has already faded. The fruit is bitter - hence the name, though like many other cherries the bark is useful as a sedative and a tonic infusion

Bird cherry initiates a healing balance and an increase in happiness. There is a noticeable relaxation, particularly of body-awareness and an increased sensuality.

The Gall Bladder meridian is cleansed of tension created by a sense of self-righteousness. This increases sense of humour and a more tolerant understanding of the self, one's potential, and acceptance of the possibility for self-healing.

Emotional indifference is eased. There can be deep healing of those emotional wounds, which the outer show of indifference is intended to protect or disguise. Self-criticism and guilt relates to the functions of the Large Intestine meridian and this is energised and balanced with bird cherry. Healing arises when there is a connection of the self to the rest of creation, with the understanding that it is necessary to love and be loved. Feelings of unworthiness, guilt and self-disgust can be dissolved.

The emotional body is freed to enable it to judge more fairly, to see clearly and to communicate true feelings. The mental body can be cleared of negative self-beliefs, increasing the available life-energy and allowing forgiveness.

Signature: The abundant, strongly scented flowers (almond-like, cyanogenous compounds), displayed in instantly recognisable spikes suggest self- awareness and pleasure in physical existence. An abundance of expression.

Comment: The stalks of all species of cherry can be infused in water to act as an astringent and tonic. Cherry stalks help bronchial complaints, anaemia and diarrhoea.

Black Poplar
(Populus nigra)

Key: SOLIDITY; COMPLETE SECURITY; PLACE OF CALM
PEACE; FINE PERCEPTIONS; VIEW FROM THE STILL
CENTRE; INDIGO.

Most black poplars in Britain are hybrid varieties planted for
rapid growth and effective windbreaks. The true native black
poplar is one of the most endangered species in Britain today
with only a thousand or so recorded. It can be identified by its
birch-like leaves (hybrids have longer and more heart-shaped
leaves), and by the rough, heavily burred trunk. Poplars cross-
breed easily so exact identification can be difficult. Large male
catkins appear in March, a deep red colour. Female trees
produce a yellow catkin that elongates to become necklace-like
fruit that release large amounts of cotton fine seeds in June.
Black poplar is a large spreading tree with thick branches that
can reach 100 feet (30 m).

The key for black poplar is solidity and security. It brings about
an inner environment where peace can be established as a
powerful state. Consciousness is raised to a level of detachment
where the reality of situations are recognised from a spiritual,
unifying viewpoint. At its finest, this essence brings in
universal wisdom and a sense of complete security, at home
even in the velvet depths of space.

The thymus gland is activated which strengthens the immune
responses. Self-confidence and life-energy also increase.
Chakras at the brow and throat are stimulated together with
the 11th chakra which is located above the head quite some
distance from the physical body. This allows fine perceptions
and discernment to become integrated with normal behaviour
patterns.

89

Black Poplar

A link is created between the etheric body and the soul body. This brings spiritual energies closer towards the physical body increasing the sense of confidence and security. The Heart meridian is balanced, increasing the acceptance of love and forgiveness.

Signature: The deep roots are well known for their ability to search out water sources from a great distance.

Comment: Black poplar is so-named from the deep shadows cast by the knotted, burred and gnarled trunk. The commonly seen Lombardy poplar is an upright, narrow variety of black poplar thought to have originated in Asia and brought to Britain from northern Italy in 1758. The core energy to the native tree is quite similar, as is that of the hybrids, though superficial characteristics tend to modify the expressions of that energy: hybrids have a much lighter, airier feel, whilst Lombardy poplars are more densely foliated and have a powerful verticality that can be perceived as an energy flow far into the air above the tree. From a distance poplars are easy to identify as their large leaves silhouette separately against the sky giving a stippled effect.

Blackthorn

Blackthorn
(Prunus spinosa)

Key: CIRCULATION OF ENERGY; ROOTING SPIRIT INTO MATTER; OPTIMISM; PROTECTION FROM NEGATIVITY; FORCE OF NEW LIFE; RED.

Blackthorn is commonly found in hedgerows and at the edge of scrub woodland. Each plant suckers freely to produce dense masses of impenetrable thornbushes. Blackthorn can become a small tree but never grows much more than 15 feet (4m). It has black, shiny bark with strong sharp spines and a hard orange wood - traditionally the material of cudgels ("shillelagh") because of its heaviness and strength. The densely packed white flowers open in spring before the small leaves appear. The earliest white blossom in the British countryside is cherry plum, followed by blackthorn, then wild cherry in April, then hawthorn in May. The fruits, "sloes", are blue-black and very sour, becoming fully ripened after the first frosts.

There is an energising of the physical body with this essence. It can be of use to help improve the oxygenation of cells and to improve the efficiency of the blood supply. This can increase the amount of nutrition available to the body. Because of these qualities blackthorn can be helpful with migraine, PMT, menstrual cramps and poor circulation.

Hope and joy increases with the lively energising of the Small Intestine and Triple Warmer meridians.

The base chakra (survival issues, manifestation, physical skill), and the heart chakra (balancing, integrating, understanding) are positively influenced. A small chakra at the base of the arch of the foot which relates to the functions of the small intestine, is stimulated and this helps the absorption of various minerals that stabilise emotional states. The emotions are not strongly affected by blackthorn except when they directly relate to energy levels, chemical balances and nutrition. In these cases other appropriate essences may be one of the maples (Silver, Field, Sycamore). The increase of energy levels helps to counter the effects of sadness, solitude and hopelessness.

Blackthorn is a very protective essence particularly from non-physical entities and energy patterns that may weaken or infiltrate the subtle spiritual body. There is an overall spiritualisation and integration of fine level energy, a rooting of the spirit into matter.

Signature: The white frosting of blackthorn across the countryside in early spring is sign of returning energy and life to the land. The sharp, spiky thorns emphasise the here-and-now of physical existence. The velvety-purple sloes: spirit growing from the energy of form.

Comment: Blackthorn epitomises the delicacy and strength of the force of life. The spirit of blackthorn we once saw as a young warrior girl guided and perhaps guarded by a surly looking, cudgel-wielding dwarf.

Box
(Buxus sempevirens)

Key: CLARITY; FLOW OF POSITIVE ENERGY; CLEANSING AND CALMING; UNBLOCKING; PURIFICATION; PERSONAL ENERGY INTEGRITY; WHITE.

A few groves of box exist on the chalk and limestone of the North Downs, Chilterns and Cotswolds. Its heavy dense wood is the only native wood that, when green, sinks in water. Being heavily cropped for its timber, few large mature trees now exist in the wild. It can grow to a height of 35 feet (11m). Box has small, dark evergreen leaves and a smooth, finely cracked light brown bark. The yellow flowers appear in April at the leaf axils, each cluster containing up to five male flowers surrounding a central female flower.

Box is a useful essence to stimulate the immune system and the quality of life-energy within the individual. This is particularly appropriate where emotions are involved. Sorrow, disappointment and grief are known to seriously deplete the natural immunity to disease, and this is often why so many people become seriously run-down soon after suffering a significant sadness in their life. Box helps to sustain the flow of positive energy and optimistic view of life.

This process can reduce the tendency of becoming physically blocked - such as in the sinuses of the head and in the cleansing action of the kidneys. There is a calming effect that may sometimes prove useful with inflammations and irritation such as hayfever and other immune system over-reactions.

The Stomach meridian is stimulated and will more effectively cleanse and repair issues of negative self-image, particularly to do with belief systems where there is conflict between desires

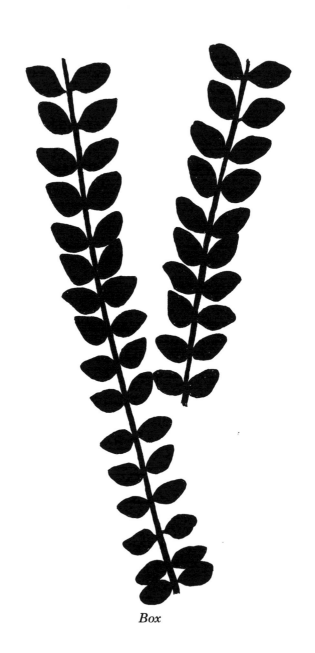

Box

and feelings of disgust and dirtiness. Understanding and letting go of old conflicts is made possible.

The causal body, connecting self to the collective soul of humanity, is also given healing. There will be an increased feeling of connectedness to the energy of the universe and a reduction of feelings of separation, isolation and unworthiness.

When these false concepts begin to be removed extra energy can be redirected to mental and spiritual states. So there is an increase in energy levels and more constructive activity. Strong feelings can now be focused in creative, helpful ways and a greater spiritual maturity can emerge.

Box can also be used as a way to purify and cleanse the atmosphere, both on a physical level as well as from negative or dulling thought-forms and spirit energies.

Signature: The finest and hardest of native timbers, box was used almost exclusively for woodblock engraving, being stable and very hard-wearing. The signature of maintaining its integrity under pressure. The yellow wood suggests confidence and positivity of the solar plexus chakra. The leaf is notched at the end as if the box energies are turning back inwards on themselves - again conserving and maintaining personal energy status.

Comment: Box wood was formerly powdered and together with the leaves was used as a powerful purgative. It was also used to treat both people and animals suffering from parasite infestation. In lesser doses box is a sedative. Very few box hedges are seen in flower unless they have been left to grow out naturally for a while. There are many varieties of box for use in hedging.

Catalpa

Catalpa
(Catalpa x erubescans)

Key: JOY; INCREASE OF PEACE; STABILISING EMOTIONS; BALANCE AND DISCRIMINATION; RESOLUTION OF CONFLICTS; YELLOW-GREEN.

The catalpa, also called the Indian bean tree, is named from the native American tribe, the Catawba of the Louisiana and Florida regions. Catalpas are sensitive to frost so they are usually only found in the south of Britain. They come into leaf very late in June, and flower in August or September. Flowers appear on large spikes, somewhat similar to horse chestnut "candles", but more open. The hybrid catalpa, a cross between the southern catalpa and the yellow catalpa from China, was introduced into Britain in 1891 and has a sweet, powerful scent. In winter the tree is characterised by its long, bean-like seed pods, in summer by its huge leaves.

The quality of catalpa is primarily in the increase of peace and the calming of anxieties. There is a stabilisation of the emotions.

The Small Intestine meridian is supported. This is the channel that becomes stressed by sadness and sorrow, and energised by joy and happiness. There is a general calming of the emotions and of the energy pulses at various parts of the body. Very often these pulses can be felt to be out of synchrony when a person is under stress, falling back into rhythm as the stress is lifted. Catalpa essence placed on these pulse points (like the wrists, the frontal eminences on the forehead and the tops of the little fingers), would help to regulate these subtle energies very quickly.

As the body calms down the mind can achieve a new state of balance and discrimination. The energies of this tree are largely focused on balancing the polarity of the intuition and the intellect, the personal wants with the appropriate needs, the flow of personal expression and will, and the balance of happiness and fear.

The lifting of conflicts, both emotional and mental, can lead to a greater sense of security and connectedness into the surroundings and even an increased ability to use psychic and other skills in a useful way.

Signature: The tree remains dormant and at peace for much of the year - when it comes into life it does so with exuberance and abundance. The long purple bean pods may suggest the channels through which the subtle pulses can be felt.

Comment: There are several mature hybrid catalpas planted around Exeter. For most of the year they remain inconspicuous until they come into magnificently huge leaf and then later infuse their surroundings with the light, sweet, complex scent of their flowers.

Cedar of Lebanon
(Cedrus libani)

Key: TURMOIL; CONFUSION; DESPAIR; TAKING A DEEP BREATH; UNDERSTANDING; QUIET ENOUGH TO HEAR; GREEN.

This familiar parkland tree is characterised by its dark green foliage arranged in flat planes on horizontal branches. Male flowers release pollen in autumn fertilising small female flowers that become barrel-shaped cones. This cedar, with strong, durable, aromatic wood was used so much in ancient shipbuilding and temple construction that the huge forests of the Levant were destroyed leaving the arid, desert conditions of today. It was introduced into Britain in 1636.

At physical levels there is a cleansing within the respiratory system. This also occurs with the use of the cedar's essential oil.

There is, overall, a quietening of emotional turmoil. A reduction in mental and emotional friction encourages a deep peacefulness that can reveal one's own foundation of peace.

When there is confusion and despair this essence brings a wordless understanding. There is relaxation, acceptance and a lessening of any resistance to necessary change. With this letting go there is the ability to hear clearer messages from the deep mind and the universe regarding appropriate actions.

Signature: The visual stability and sense of balance: strong-boughed, level-headed. The aromatic scent is warm, relaxing and preserving.

Cedar of Lebanon

Cherry Laurel
(Prunus laurocerasus)

Key: BALANCE OF MIND; HEAD; ORGANISATION OF INTERNAL HARMONY; QUIET MIND; SUBTLE PERCEPTION; INSIGHT; BLUE-ORANGE.

This is the well-known laurel used for hedging since its introduction into Britain in 1576. It is, in fact, a bird cherry of the prunus family originating from around the Caspian and Black Sea. In the past its major use was in creating a dense ground and woodland cover for game birds. Tolerant of shade and moisture it can be very invasive and its shiny evergreen foliage can reach up to 20ft (6m) - though it can be quite startling to see cherry laurel as a tree in its own right, rather than a clipped hedge. The flower spikes are visible early in spring around April, giving off a heady sweet scent from the creamy yellow flowers. Like all cherries this laurel contains a high proportion of prussic acid and when the leaves are crushed they give off the distinctive almond scent of hydrocyanic acid. The flowers ripen to shiny black berries eaten by birds.

The essence focuses on bringing balance to the mental activities and it can be used whenever there is trauma to the head. It will quickly release shock, even from near-death experiences.

Cherry laurel allows imagination to be used in a constructive way, enabling more of one's personal potential to be expressed. Imagination and inspiration is greatly enhanced.

At genetic and molecular levels cherry laurel's energy helps to maintain and balance an individual's evolutionary development in an organised, intelligent manner. The intelligence and organising power of molecular structures and genetic material is upheld to allow for maximum evolutionary progress. It may

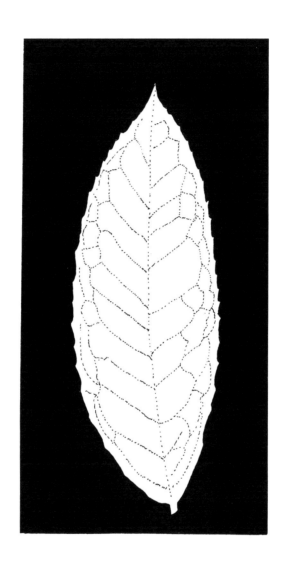

Cherry Laurel

be possible that harmful compounds like free radicals and errors in the genetic material can be reduced. Primarily cherry laurel works to achieve this by regulating the belief structures and fine level energy flows of the mental and spiritual bodies where such difficulties would first appear, as energy dissonance.

The brow chakra is energised in a way that quietens mental activity to such a degree that a depth and clarity of subtle perceptions and insights are able to be identified. This can help with all forms of spiritual communication and channelling. This is also aided by the activation of the crown chakra where the finest levels of the self are linked more closely to the underlying universal sources. This allows an influx of universal harmony, connectedness and fine spiritual energy into the self. The energy link is inherently protective, non-aggressive and supportive, and in this way all aspects of the mind can be made whole, holistic and healed.

Signature: The "heady" scent; and the erect spikes like aerials, or reminiscent of the higher energy centres on and above the head.

Comment: It is easy to ignore the trees that have become associated with the domestic and suburban environments, but these are the ones to which many people have the most familiar links - albeit mostly unconscious. It is all too common for these trees to be despised as "introductions", non-natives, weeds, as though they contain less of value than other kingdoms. Such prejudices should be looked out for in oneself and counteracted by conscious acknowledgement and experience of their spirit energies. It was, after all, humans who decided to bring these particular species closer to our own. This necessitates respect and understanding. Such beliefs, whether of other species or amongst our own, are significant energy drains and show fundamental lack of understanding of the web of creation as a unified equality of individuality.

It is interesting to note that cherry laurel's introduction coincides with the English Renaissance when the mind, both rational and imaginative, became the main instrument for investigating both the sciences and the arts.

Cherry laurel's native homeland is one of the areas of great importance in the cultural origins of the Old European cultures.

Cheɹɹy Plum
(*Prunus cerasifera*)

Key: CONFIDENCE; SHYNESS OVERCOME; REMOVAL OF FEARS; THROAT CHAKRA; STRONG EMOTIONS; TRUE FEELINGS; SERENITY; PEACE; ORANGE-BLUE.

Also called the myrobalan plum, it is a semi-wild little tree originally from eastern Europe and Central Asia. It is the earliest white blossom to appear in the hedgerows and can be distinguished from blackthorn as the flowers are usually more sparse and delicate with a touch of green from the young leaf-shoots. Cherry plum flowers in February or early March and can grow to be an open-crowned spreading tree of 25 ft. (7.5 m).

A purple-leaved variety, *"Pissardii"*, is commonly planted in gardens. This is a natural sport that arose in the Shah of Persia's gardens in the late 19th century and was sent to France. It has pinkish flowers.

The essence of cherry plum helps to remove fears and anxiety by uncovering the wisdom and ultimate security of the inner self. Tensions that are locked into the muscle system relating to such fears and mental attitude can be eased.

The Central meridian (Conception Vessel) strengthens to improve self-confidence. This combats shyness and brings about a space to develop a fuller personal potential.

The throat chakra is energised and enabled to make practical use of subtle perceptions, intuition, inspiration and so on. Communication and artistic blocks are eased. At the same time the crown chakra becomes clearer allowing more healing, universal energies to merge and harmonise with the localised identity of the self at a safe rate and pace. The sense of time

107

Cherry Plum

and space is relaxed so that the present comes into better focus and can be honestly experienced as it is.

As well as this connection with stabilising universal energies cherry plum also allows a better connection with others at an emotional, feeling level. This helps to balance the emotions and suggests that cherry plum would be useful for those who are affected by strong emotional swings.

Mentally this tree essence brings a deep peace and serenity, quietening the heart and mind and allowing the inner self to come through.

Comment: Cherry plum was one of Edward Bach's flower remedies indicated for those with dammed-up anger that overflows into violent rage at the slightest provocation, or for those who feared that dramatic and destructive release. The qualities described here emphasise the ability to relax and allow energy to flow, thus avoiding the dangerous build-up.

Copper Beech

Copper Beech
(Fagus sylvatica var. purpurea)

Key: DEPRESSION; REVEALING PATTERNS OF BEHAVIOUR; DETACHMENT FROM PAST; HUMOUR; CLARITY; JOY.

Copper beech was first recorded as growing in Switzerland in 1680 and later also arose at least a couple of times in Germany. Its form and habit is identical to the common green variety except that its foliage has a deep reddish-purple colour. Copper beech is mainly found as a garden or park tree where its colour stands out dramatically amongst the surrounding vegetation.

The emotions are energised, but in a positive way. Anger and repressed, or otherwise inappropriate, emotions are expelled in a non-aggressive, positive way. There is a greater under-standing and acceptance of the individual's deep unconscious emotional tendencies and instincts - the patterns of behaviour that automatically trigger in certain situations. Emotional difficulties with relationships are eased. Copper beech helps to see each situation as it is, rather than being viewed through a distorting screen of past experience.

There is the possibility to relieve depression and bring a deep, enlivening sense of peace and detachment from worries as stress is lifted from these aspects of the Lung meridian. The emotional body becomes better balanced giving a sense of easiness and humour. There is a more relaxed ability to accept and express lovingly who one is and what one feels.

There is a greater positive receptivity: an ability to be peaceful without a need to do something else. It can be useful in depression or when there is need for greater emotional independence or detachment from an emotional situation.

At extremely fine, universal levels this tree helps to sharpen intelligence, clarity and the sense of joy.

Signature: The purple-red leaves appear sombre and weighty yet allow a red light to filter through. This feels quietening and energising. Magenta, pink and red are the qualities of this essence together with an indigo-purple.

Comment: The colour of a plant's leaves is an indication of the energies that it does not absorb from sunlight. Hence green leaved plants reflect green light favouring the reds, yellows, blues and violets. Copper beech reflects dark reds and blue-blacks. It absorbs almost the opposite frequencies of light to green leaves absorbing much more of the mid-spectrum range. Energetically and metaphysically, copper beech is thus an interesting tree spirit to explore.

CRack Willow
(Salix fragilis)

Key: SPIRITUAL SUN; FLEXIBILITY; LET THINGS BE;
VITALITY; CONTENTMENT; SOLAR LOGOS; YELLOW.

Just about a quarter of the native species of British trees are
willows. Whether native or introduced, all species interbreed
freely often making precise identification difficult. Crack willow
is one of the largest species growing to between 30 and 40 ft. It
has a wide, open crown, often with several trunks spreading
outwards from the base, and a rough, thick-ridged bark. It can
be identified from its leaves which are long, thin blades with
fine serrated edges ending in a long point. When touched or
bent this willow's small twigs will easily break with an audible
crack - hence the tree's name. This quality allows twigs to float
downstream where they can easily root in mud and form new
colonies.

Crack willow essence increases communication with the Higher
Self, often by stimulating the functions of the throat chakra.
The area of the throat and upper chest is also energised
particularly in respect of the immune system functions of the
thyroid and thymus glands.

Muscle tone can improve, particularly affecting the diaphragm.
Breathing may become deeper and conditions such as hiatus
hernia may ease.

There is an increased flexibility on mental and spiritual levels.
This allows the individual to be content to let things be, for
things to happen in their own good time, to let go. With this
comes the ability to look at oneself and accept what is seen.

Crack Willow

A connection is created with compassionate energies at fine levels of consciousness, and this brings a sense of oneness with the world and all beings in it. Also there is created a stronger link to the planet itself, and through this, to the place from which Earth receives its sustaining energies - that is, the sun. Crack willow particularly links to the higher vibrations of the sun's energies that have been personified as the Solar Logos, which is, as it were, the parent and creator of the whole solar system.

This essence can be used to stimulate and awaken physical vitality as it begins to flag throughout the day.

Signature: The ability to let go of parts of oneself (the twigs) in the knowledge that they will find a home elsewhere.

Comment: Willows are often associated with water, the moon and the dark aspects of the Goddess but they carry as many solar characteristics as lunar. Firstly they have a great force of growth. In winter and early spring willows stand out with their bright orange-yellow twigs and yellow male catkins - especially in bright sunlight.

Essences made from different species of willow all have a common, solar, theme. They all, in one way or another, work at revealing and expressing the true nature of the self.

Elder

Elōer
(Sambucus nigra)

Key: SELF-WORTH; CALM; STABILITY; TRANSFORMS AGGRESSION; TOLERANCE AND LOVE; FRETFUL CHILDREN; PINK.

Elder can be found wherever the soil is rich in nitrogen - near abandoned houses, in churchyards, where there is dung and refuge. The breakdown of organic matter frees up this nitrogen for the plants to use. Elder grows vigorously and colonises an area very rapidly. It usually remains a bush but with enough space and light can grow into a small tree up to 30ft. (9m). Elder is probably Britain's smelliest tree - the leaves have a distinctive sharp pungency which becomes a delicious creamy sweetness in the large umbels of flowers that open in May and June. The elderberries, blue-black and numerous, are edible, nutritious and tasty. In fact, elder is one of the most useful hedgerow plants. It provides food, dyes, medicines and alcoholic beverages. The wood is hard enough to be a substitute for boxwood but elder has a large pithy core that limits the size of useful pieces. Elder comes into leaf very early - green shoots begin to be seen in February.

Elder primarily is a calming and stabilising essence. Aggression in any form, outward or inner, can be directed or transformed. Fears and anxieties are eased. There is a greater understanding and acceptance, a clearer insight into one's emotional reactions. Elder brings an increase of tolerance, love and forgiveness. This has a positive effect on the Lung meridian, clearing from that energy channel blocks caused by scorn, intolerance, prejudice and haughtiness, increasing the qualities of humility, tolerance and modesty.

Solar plexus, heart and brow chakras are strengthened. Here there is an increase in calm and an ability to receive communication from deep intuitive levels. There is greater consideration of options before actions are taken - so can be helpful for the reckless or careless.

The essence can be helpful for all issues of understanding, self-worth and self-esteem. It gives support in times of transformation and change, giving flexibility and creativity to resolve and repair self-damaging beliefs.

Elder is a useful essence for children, particularly fretful babies and toddlers.

Signature: From the buried remains, the detritus, the dead, springs a tree of great value in healing.

Comment: Elder is widely connected to the death aspect of the Goddess in European tradition. "Elder Moeder" is the female/male wildfolk tree spirit whose permission should be sought before anything is taken from the tree.

English Elm
(*Ulmus procera*)

Key: ENTHUSIASM; FINE LEVELS OF INFORMATION; UNDERSTANDING; OVERVIEW; PRACTICALITY; CONFUSION AND FATIGUE EASES; DRAINED AND OVER-EMOTIONAL STATES; YELLOW-BLUE.

There are many varieties of elm with very similar forms. Each tends to have a quite clearly defined location. English elm predominated in the hedgerows of the Midlands and southern England. The Cornish elm is either native or an early introduction and remains dominant in the far west. The Wheatley or Jersey elm is a variety of the smooth-leaved elm found on the Continent and more frequent in the eastern and southern counties of England.

The English elm was characterised by its tall, narrow crown with dense foliage growing close to the boughs. It could reach a height of 120 ft. (36m). All elms, except wych elm, sucker freely and even with the continuing ravages of Dutch elm disease hedgerows still contain many young elms ,easily identified by their vigorous growth at a regular angle of about 45 degrees to the main trunk and the clearly alternate large leaves. The flowers are small and appear on the twigs early in the year well before the leaves appear, giving the whole tree a reddish tinge. The ripening seed cases are a vivid light -green mass of leaf-like ovals hanging in great profusion from the branches. It is thought by some that the distribution of English elm suggests it was brought into the country by the pre-Celtic peoples.

The essence of elm brings the ability to organise fine levels of information or energy in a way that can be easily understood. It allows a greater ability to have an overview of any situation,

English Elm

giving discrimination and sufficient detachment. There is also the possibility of knowledge from the beyond.

When there is a lack of perspective and loss of control - such as in hysteria - the regulating Circulation-sex (Pericardium) meridian is given greater stability. Practicality dominates over flights of imaginative possibility.

The Large Intestine meridian is also affected with an increased ability to cleanse and remove foreign materials by establishing correct sense of personal boundaries, increased sense of purpose and direction. Clarification of who one is allows identification of what one wishes to distance oneself from.

Elm brings the ability to experience and understand others on a level of feeling. Emotions are stabilised. There is an increase in equilibrium and compassion and the ability to give and receive love. It also becomes possible to determine more accurately the validity of personal actions, balancing the qualities of conscience and guilt feelings. Many chakras around the heart and abdomen are brought into balance. The brow chakra, too, is boosted creating a dynamic calm that allows experience of fine perception and transcendence of normal states of consciousness.

Confusion, oppression, fatigue are reduced making decisions easier. Elm is a useful essence to use to re-energise the mind when fatigued and balance the heart when feeling drained or over-emotional.

Field Maple

Fielò Maple
(Acer campestre)

Key: ACHING HEART; SAFE WITHIN SELF; BALANCE
AFTER SHOCK; RETURN TO CENTRE; HEART CHAKRA;
LOVE; PINK.

Field maple is the only maple native to Britain. It is quite
common on chalky soils but is often not very obvious though it
can grow to a tree up to 85 feet (26 metres). The leaves have
the familiar maple shape but are simpler with three main
rounded lobes. The leaves unfold a pink colour and become a
butter yellow in autumn. The small upright clusters of flowers
in spring are green and not very noticeable.

The clearest time to identify field maple in the hedgerows is
around the summer solstice when a second growth shows a
bright red. The burring and knots on the main trunk made
field maple a decorative wood until replaced by imported maple
woods.

There can be total security within the self that allows uncondit-
ional love to be given and received. Field maple acts as a
balance to those who desperately seek love without looking
inside themselves to discover what may be pushing that love
away. Once achieved inside, love will appear wherever one
looks. This essence draws down a high wisdom energy from
above the crown chakra and helps to establish it in the solar
plexus chakra where it is able to manifest its power.

Physically, field maple can ease the respiratory system and
blood flow, mainly through a deep relaxation and clarification of
energy use.

There is understanding and contentment for those who are overwhelmed by remorse or a sense of being responsible for events and accidents. It can rebalance after shock. Field maple enables one to return to centre.

It opens and balances the heart chakra allowing an expansion of the awareness of relationships to others and being part of an integrated universal web of interaction and growth. The consciousness of universal love.

Emotional problems are calmed, especially where there is anger or over-aggression. This is because field maple balances the love aspects of the self.

At the finest levels of energy this tree establishes a line from the absolute, indefinable levels of creation, the void, to that place where boundaries and the relative levels of existence begin to emerge. When this region becomes familiar it links one to an infinite source of awareness and power where self and universe merge.

Gean (Wild Cherry)
(Prunus avium)

Key: SOOTHING; TIMES OF TRANSITION; PAIN; FREE FLOW OF ENERGY; CALM; RECONNECTING WITH THE PHYSICAL; COMPASSION; PINK.

The gean or mazzard is a native British cherry of woodlands that grows to 80 feet (25m.). In April and May clusters of white flowers emerge from chubby terminal buds before the leaves are fully out. Gean is the original stock from which domestic cherries derive, though most of the wild fruit is taken by animals and birds. The bark is characteristically shiny red-brown with horizontal banding. Cherry wood is compact, fine-grained and heavy. All green parts of the tree have a high content of hyocyanic acid that helps protect from predation.

Gean helps one to let go of unwanted patterns of behaviour, particularly where there is a problem with self-image such as during times of illness. This essence will help with transitions of all kinds.

Sacral and solar plexus chakra are released from stress, again focusing where there are damaging or negative self-beliefs to do with sensuality, sexuality, creativity and physicality.

Gean has a soothing effect. It seems to increase the effectiveness of the body's natural painkillers, the endorphins and similar molecules, and so can prove useful where there is pain, inflammation and irritation. Energy tends to be focused into the physical system and thus stimulate self-healing. This energy flow enters smoothly into the subtle nervous system and helps to balance the whole system. As the channels are cleared the sensation of pain is naturally reduced (pain is the body's indication of a concentration or block of flow).

125

Gean - Wild Cherry

With gean it is possible to begin the process of purification and cleansing that allows growth and change into one's life. There can be a new clarity that arises from a greater understanding of self-compassion and acceptance. With this calm and clarity there can be an increase of psychic skills, including the perception of subtle beings and access to ancient wisdom.

Signature: The sweetness of the fruit arises from the bitter astringency of leaves and twigs. The non-green parts of the tree, that is those parts not containing the acid, are traditionally used to make soothing, pain-reducing remedies.

Comment: Wild cherry tree spirit can be one of the most useful energies from which to ask aid wherever there is fear caused by disease or illness. The spirit re-establishes a caring, life-supporting contact with the physical which is often denied support by the fearful mind.

Giant Redwood

Giant Redwood
(Giant Sequoia, Wellingtonia)
(Sequoiadedron giganteum)

Key: WEIGHT OF RESPONSIBILITY; ABDOMEN; TOO HARD ON SELF AND OTHERS; CLEAR DECISION MAKING; FLEXIBLE COMMUNICATION; CREATIVITY; GREEN-ORANGE.

This tree, native only to the inland slopes of the Sierra Nevada mountain range in central California, is the largest tree in the world. The circumference of the base of the trunk can reach 200ft. Younger trees have characteristic downswept branches that are usually shed in mature trees of well over 3,000 years old. It has a deep green, rounded crown of scaly, sharp-pointed leaves growing to 250 ft. Flowers are small cone-like developments on branch endings.

The first seeds were sent to Britain in 1853, the year the Duke of Wellington died. Disease resistant and wind-firm, it quickly became a feature of estates and gardens.

Giant redwood essence helps to balance, tone and relax the muscles of the abdomen and pelvic regions. It can also help the circulation in the hands and feet.

The Bladder meridian is brought to a better balance helpful to identify direction in life; the Lung meridian is helped to increase tolerance; the Gall Bladder to increase the sense of love and forgiveness. It thus helps those who can be too hard on themselves and on others.

Activity is focused at the sacral and throat chakras. Relaxation that allows energy to flow and clear decisions to be made. There is an increase of flexibility in methods of communication and a greater moderation and appreciation of personal desires, both in oneself and others.

There is a greater chance of balancing mundane and spiritual values, and of balancing relationship of self to the outside world. Whether this concerns over-involvement with others or an inability to share, giant redwood will achieve a workable balance that reduces the stress of such situations.

The mental body is cleared of blocks to creativity and to understanding. Fixed, outmoded belief systems, which tend to create frozen or fixed muscle tension, are eased and so the muscles are helped to relax.

Signature: The ability of older trees to lose unnecessary weight by shedding lower branches.

Glastonbury Thorn
(Crataegus monogyna biflora)

Key: OUT OF THE WOODS; STAGNANT ENERGY; PERSONAL PATH; INTUITION AND ADVICE; CLARITY OF PURPOSE; ABILITY TO REACH GOALS; HEART; SELF-AWARENESS; GREEN-GOLD.

The Glastonbury thorn is probably one of the world's best known trees, so closely linked has it become with the legends of early Christianity, King Arthur and the Grail that surrounds this small Somerset town. The original tree was reputed to have sprung from the staff of Joseph of Arimathaea who rested here whilst carrying the Grail of Christ's blood, and who is said to have chosen Glastonbury as the site of the first church in Britain.

The tree itself has had a chequered history, being the focus of spite for religious fundamentalists of one sort or another, nevertheless cuttings have kept the tree and its legend alive. The thorn is thought to be a type of hawthorn found in the eastern Mediterranean, which explains its habit of flowering not only in summer (a little later than common hawthorns), but also around midwinter.

The essence of Glastonbury thorn can help to remove stagnant energy from the circulation and the area of the heart and lungs. This is not so much a physical cleansing as a clearing of subtle energy blocks.

The heart chakra is greatly strengthened. Relaxing and opening up the energy centre, a sense of great weight being lifted from the heart as if a new path opens up before you at a time where all seems to be turmoil and confusion.

Glastonbury Thorn

At the level of the emotions a peace emerges that allows movement in the right direction for the individual's own path. This same calmness also clears the thought processes so that information can be understood and properly utilised.

Having achieved a clearer understanding of one's personal path ("dharma", duty, destiny, potential etc.), this sense of acceptance and relaxation allows a much deeper level of intuition and information or energy to be perceived and understood. In this state of deep peace advice as to one's "right action" can be more clearly heard.

Signature: The staff of Joseph of Arimathaea: support for the traveller, clarity of purpose, ability to reach the distant goal.

Comment: This essence has many of the characteristic energy of other hawthorns. It is very heart-centred and supportive of self-awareness. The mythic attributions carry this particular tree into higher octaves of energy resonance. Qualities of time, truth and belief - the nature of reality itself as seen through human history - weave around this small tenacious bush. Issues of personal belief, understanding one's true heart, both its desires and goals, and the nature of personal devotion can be explored through the energy pattern of Glastonbury thorn.

Gorse

Gorse

(Ulex europeus, Ulex gallica)

Key: INTEGRATION OF HEART AND MIND; SOLID GROWTH; FRUSTRATION; RESTLESSNESS; SOLAR PLEXUS; ENERGY; HOPE; INSPIRATION; GOLD.

Gorse rarely becomes large enough to be called a tree. It can grow to 7ft. (2m) even in its usual habitat of windswept heathland. The sharp spines that cover the flexible branches are in fact the plant's evergreen leaves. The coconut-scented flowers open in golden yellow profusion around the end of April, though gorse flowers can be seen throughout the year. There are several different species of gorse showing slight variations of form and time of flowering.

The main characteristic of gorse is the integration of heart and mind. This enables a synthesis of many different ideas and re-energises old, established or forgotten patterns of information in a way that proves useful to the individual outlook.

These new forms of energy/information become better integrated into the physical energy patterns from the much finer subtle bodies from which they emerge. This ensures that they are much more likely to be of practical value. As a result there is an increase in joy arising from a greater feeling of security and growth.

Gorse is particularly good at bringing the fine levels of positive energy from subtle, universal levels and fully integrating them within the emotional and feeling bodies so that they can be easily expressed in activity.

At a physical level gorse boosts the immune system, largely through its ability to enhance positivity. Specifically it may prove useful with ureter or urinary infections.

The meridians of the Bladder and Circulation-Sex (Pericardium) are strengthened. This eases restlessness, frustration and jealousy - states arising from discomfort with the individual's own situation and the seeming inability to change that situation. Some smaller chakras within the lower abdomen are also given energy, enhancing creativity, joy, inner stability, power, healing potential and balanced sexuality.

Signature: The golden flowers indicate the qualities of integration of energy, such as via the solar plexus chakras. The loud popping of seed cases on hot summer's days is reminiscent of the "lightbulb" of new ideas and inspiration.

Comment: Edward Bach used gorse for those displaying the symptoms of great hopelessness and despair, convinced that no improvement would be possible. He saw that the golden flowers brought the energy and hope of the bright sunlight into people's hearts again.

Great Sallow
(Salix caprea)

Key: SOUL; DYNAMIC MIND; ENERGISING BODY; CALM BALANCE; EXPANSION OF CONSCIOUS AWARENESS; UNDERSTANDING NEEDS OF SELF AND OTHERS; GREEN-YELLOW.

Great sallow, also known as goat willow, is a small, many-stemmed tree that can grow to 50 ft. (15m). It is the well-known "pussy-willow" with silky, silver buds on the female plants in early spring. Like all willows, male and female flowers appear on separate trees. Great sallow is one of the earliest willows to flower. The male flowers are grey becoming yellow when fully ripe with pollen, the female flowers are greenish white. A very common tree in Britain, great sallow colonises waste ground, especially damp places, woodlands, scrub and hedgerows. It will also spread onto drier soils. The bark contains tannins and salicins used in medicine (as an astringent and painkiller). The wood is light and soft. A natural hybrid, the Kilmarnock willow, is a "weeping" variety found in 1840 in Scotland.

Great sallow, like others of the willow family, is an energiser. It works to stimulate and motivate the mind in practical, dynamic ways. Both the solar plexus chakra and the eighth chakra located above the head are activated, and this creates a link with the soul through which the conscious awareness can expand. The result is a greater understanding of life purpose that leads to a release of tension. This in turn allows a greater energising of the whole body.

Extensive tension or rigidity in the knees can ease which creates a better link to earth energy.

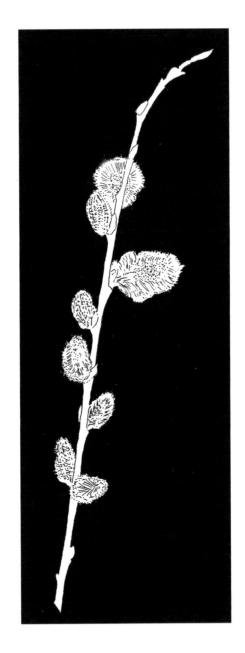

Great Sallow

The other major influence of this essence is to bring a profound calm and balance into the whole system.

The heart and Heart meridian are stimulated for greater understanding of others, and the relationship of self to others. There is a greater appreciation of the needs of others and a balanced acceptance of personal responsibility and willingness to help, without compromising personal space. Great sallow will help those who are either too involved or those who avoid relationships.

All the different aspects of the subtle self are brought into a greater harmony, and this particularly helps to remove self-defeating behaviour patterns.

The mind, the whole conscious levels of awareness and the higher spiritual energies are brought to a place of calmness and balance from which personal power and steady growth can evolve.

Hawthorn

Hawthorn
(Crataegus monogyna)

Key: LOVE; BALANCING AND REGULATING HEART CHAKRA; TRUST; FORGIVENESS; STRESS LIFTS FROM HEART; PINK- GREEN.

Hawthorn, May, quickthorn or whitethorn is one of the commonest of British trees, quickly establishing itself in both grassland and wood. Its slow growth and tangled spiny form makes it an ideal hedging plant for which it has been used down the centuries. Hawthorn flowers between late April and early June, though traditionally it signifies the quarter day of Beltane, the 1st of May, beginning of summer. The blossoms are creamy white, sometimes pink, and they lie densely along the top of the branches. The smell is sweet, musky and erotic. The ripened fruit, the red haws, can be seen colouring the trees towards the end of August. Hawthorn wood is even, fine grained and quite lovely to work with, having a soft orange-pink colour. As a herbal remedy hawthorn is one of the best heart regulators, able to normalise a variety of conditions.

Hawthorn's primary importance is as a balance and regulator of the energies of the heart chakra. The essence carries the benefit of the herbal preparation in that it will strengthen the heart in whichever direction it requires to normalise the function. Other essences and plants may be deleterious with some heart conditions, hawthorn can be used quite safely in most instances.

Hawthorn relieves stresses placed upon the heart centre - whatever the quality or origin of that stress. It increases trust and the ability to give and receive love. It brings forgiveness, particularly of the self, and helps to cleanse the heart of negativity.

The heart centre is the balance point and the centre of individual awareness. From this point the quality of the self is judged and how the self interacts and relates to all else in the world around it. The heart is the standard by which the individual weighs and interprets all experience. As such, this energy centre needs to remain clear of stress and free from inappropriate beliefs if full potential is to be achieved in life.

As the central pivot of the energy structures of the body, the heart chakra affects every other channel and centre. Hawthorn, by balancing the heart, can help to balance and align all the main energy centres.

Signature: Although appearing a gnarled and thorny tree its flowers feed many insects, birds and small animals throughout the year. Because of its thorny branches hawthorn is often associated with Christ's Passion: the messenger of love.

Comment: Hawthorn, because of its blossom and time of flowering, is closely related to the fecund aspects of the Goddess energy. It also has close folklore associations with nature spirits and fairy beings. For such a small tree (although it can grow in woodland to over 50ft), hawthorn has a strong, powerful and characteristic presence and awareness. Both berries and flowers can be used as an astringent for sore throats, as a diuretic and as a cardiac tonic.

Hazel
(Corylus avellana)

Key: SKILLS; FLOWERING OF SKILLS; WISDOM; COMMUNICATION; STUDY; BRAINFOOD; INSPIRATION; BLUE-GOLD.

Hazel is the earliest of British trees to come into flower. The long male catkins can be seen as early as January though it is usually February when they become heavy with yellow pollen. Hazel can grow to become a small tree of 30 ft, but it is more usually coppiced to harvest long, pliant rods or laid to make fast-growing hedging. It is short-lived unless kept as a coppice, then hazel can survive for over a thousand years old. The small, inconspicuous female flowers appear like small green barnacles with bright red stamens. Once ripened with wind-borne pollen they become a cluster of nuts, usually up to four together, each one enclosed in green leafy bracts.

Hazel brings the flowering of skills. It gives the ability to receive and communicate wisdom and so is excellent for both student and teacher. All forms of philosophy, teaching, information can be better assimilated and understood.

Because the mental body becomes better integrated with the physical body there is an ability to recognise those beliefs and ideas that hold the most usefulness and truth for the individual. The body's own intelligence and wisdom is involved here, which automatically brings more stability and focus into the present moment.

The throat chakra and a related centre where collar bones meet are energised. This helps to clarify emotions and clear away unwanted debris, particularly those outdated beliefs about the self and problems with egotistical behaviour patterns.

143

Hazel

Hazel provides communication doorways to many different levels of energy, particularly those relating to the spirits of earth and plants.

Signature: The nuts shaped like heads - brainfood.

Comment: It is worth working with hazel when there is any uncertainty about direction of work or when ideas fail to give the necessary answers. All forms of mind-work, from study to bardic inspiration to memorising, can be helped with this spirit energy.

Holly

Holly
(Ilex aquifolium)

Key: POWER OF PEACE; SPIRITUAL GUIDE; BALANCE OF MIND; SECURITY; INCREASED PEACE; RE-INTEGRATION AFTER DEEP SHOCK; IRRITABILITY; BLUE-YELLOW.

Few people are unable to identify the holly tree with its dark green glossy, evergreen leaves edged with sharp spikes. Holly will grow anywhere except excessively damp soil, and its well-protected leaves can withstand harsh conditions. Holly is common in hedgerows, often having been used in the past both as an effective barrier to animals and as a year-round guide for accurate siting of straight plough furrows. Male and female flowers grow on separate trees. Both bear small, waxy, white, four-petalled, sweet-scented flowers in May or early June. The fertilised female flowers swell to become the familiar red berries, loved by birds throughout the winter months.

Holly grows in woodland as an understorey tree able to tolerate low levels of light. It is very slow-growing and has a very fine, dense, white wood. Often old woodlands can be identified from the scattering of large old holly trees that would originally have been found among the more mature oaks and ashes long removed for their timber.

Holly is a spiritual guide and a balance for the mind. It helps clear away disturbances from the past that may cloud judgement. It encourages discrimination, balance and justice to develop.

Holly helps to activate and energise the control systems and the systems of intelligence - hence it boosts the endocrine and immune systems.

147

The essence can help one to deal with panic - that loss of control linked to a sense of insecurity. Loneliness, the need for others, or dissatisfaction with oneself, the need for security, is addressed, as is unhappiness, which again depends upon the sense of security, comfort and contentment. The Liver, Triple Warmer and Bladder meridians are all helped at this level.

The brow chakra is calmed. Irritability and noise at mental levels are reduced. Deep peace is given a chance to surface and communication processes are improved. This reduces friction in the system, calming everything right down. Eye, ear and head problems may benefit from holly essence.

There is better appreciation of the quality of life-energy within the body, and this allows a more accurate picture of safety and risk in one's surroundings, increasing the ability to be flexible and cope with situations, turning them to one's advantage.

The higher subtle bodies become better integrated which releases tension and allows deep healing and creativity to flourish. This new spiritual re-integration can effectively remove deep-seated spiritual trauma and shock.

Signature: The sharp leaves are protective of the clusters of white flowers and red fruit.

Holm Oak

(Quercus ilex)

Key: NEGATIVE EMOTIONS; THWARTED PERSONAL EXPRESSION; PERSONAL POWER; COMPETANCE; STABILITY.

The holly oak, or holm oak, is native to southern Europe. It has deep green evergreen leaves, slightly spiny when young, with paler undersides. It is a neat, dense looking tree often with multiple large boughs with the characteristic brown bark cracked into neat rectangles. It is rather sombre-looking except where new growth appears in early summer a lighter yellow-green, and a little later the long yellow catkins cover the tree.The acorns are rounder and more enclosed in their cups than the native oaks. Holm oak can grow to about 90ft. (27m.) and is often planted on exposed or seaward locations as it withstands salt winds and hot, dry conditions. It was introduced to Britain around 1500.

The essence focuses on the energy of personal space and personal expression. By activating personal creativity and a desire to assert oneself in a positive way in order to increase peace and harmony, holm oak helps to eliminate restlessness, impatience, frustration and all emotions that relate to thwarted expression. Thus negative feelings of anger, envy, greed and jealousy are dissolved. This directly strengthens the Bladder meridian allowing all such emotional disruptions and dissonances to be integrated and balanced into the system as a whole.

Holm oak helps to express personal power. There is a release of tension around the chest and back areas, and also in the lower abdomen as emotional and mental stresses are eased.

149

Holm Oak

The sacral chakra is given greater energy and this helps to stabilise the life-energy in the body, also enhancing the sense of security and issues of worthiness and competence. This in turn allows the ego to become better aligned to the higher levels of consciousness within the individual.

Signature: The dark solidity of the tree emphasises its ability to calm and stabilise. The evergreen leaves suggest a continuity and stability of energy flow.

Hornbeam

Hornbeam
(Carpinus betulus)

Key: RIGHT ACTION; CORE BEHAVIOUR PATTERNS; SELF-AWARENESS; DECISION-MAKING; ASSUREDNESS; OPPORTUNITIES; ORANGE.

This tree is native to south-east England where hornbeam woodland still exists in places. Elsewhere it has been widely planted for timber and hedging. Hornbeam looks similar to beech though the trunks are often fluted - rarely smooth and round like beech- and the leaves, though a similar colour, are narrower and more rigid with a stronger point and a distinct pleated surface. Hornbeam flowers in spring with both male catkins of green and female flowers at the end of branches emerging from young leaves with green bracts surrounding bright red styles. These ripen to form nutlets held within a three-lobed bract clustering at the end of branches.

Hornbeam means "hard wood" and it is one of the hardest and strongest of timbers formerly used for cogwheels, cutting blocks and wheel axles before iron became generally available. Though the tree can grow to be 100ft. (30m), few old trees of this size survive as it was regularly pollarded or coppiced for its poles.

Hornbeam essence creates the opportunity to clear those stresses that obscure our awareness of how we can achieve the greatest benefit from life.

A flow of energy is created deep within the cellular organism that can stimulate under-energised or stagnant areas and speed up internal communication systems. With these deep levels available core belief systems and prime emotional stances can be transformed and directed towards a more dynamic, evolutionary and creative functioning.

At the same time an increase of self-awareness and a sense of joy enables greater balance, harmony and growth. This can lead to clearer and more appropriate decision-making.

Energy centres that integrate individual consciousness with the flows within the rest of creation allow personal desires and actions to become more successful. Less effort is expended in reaching one's goals.

The Heart, Kidney and Triple Warmer meridians are affected and this helps to increase self-worth, creative security and the ability to serve within a collective framework.

Anxiety and tension within the solar plexus chakra releases enabling a new creative balance of the mind and emotions, and this, too, increases the joy of life.

Hornbeam also clears away trauma from the deep energy systems of the body, particularly when these have been instigated through speaking out against consensus views. When personal expression has been repressed or censored hornbeam works at the throat chakra to increase confidence in speaking out and simultaneously grounds spiritual knowledge so that it can be of use.

Hornbeam relates to cosmic power and energy as it manifests on the physical level.

Signature: The hard wood becomes a pivot for dynamic activity - the hub of a wheel supporting the separate spokes.

Comment: Edward Bach used this essence where people felt they lacked the ability or strength to succeed, or simply lacked energy, though would still manage to finish their tasks.

Horse Chestnut
(Aesculus hippocastanum)

Key: AGITATION; BLUE; FLOW OF INFORMATION; REDUCTION OF FRICTION; CALM; CLARITY; PEACE; STEADY, CALM MIND.

Horse chestnut could be found throughout central Europe before the last Ice Age but retreated to the high, moist valleys of the Balkan peninsula where it remained until the Turks took it to Istanbul in 1569. The tree was finally introduced into Britain in 1629. Horse chestnut is one of the largest flowering trees of the temperate world, its symmetrical, domed crown of hand-like leaves reaching to over 100 ft. (35m). The gnarled branches sweep upwards, then down, then up again at the tips. The trunk is usually short and thick, always with a spiral to the right. Its wood is soft, easily worked but not strong enough for much significant timber uses, so it is primarily planted for its magnificent candles of white flowers in late spring. Although trees can live for 300 years the average life-span is half that time.

The outer skin of the "conker" fruit contains saponin, which is used in sun-shields as it blocks ultraviolet light. The bark is effective for sluggish circulation, weak blood vessels and haemorrhoids.

The primary energy of the essence focuses on spiritual peace and the flow of intuition and information from one level to another. It provides the ability to utilise and accept transpersonal information, and from the Higher self for example.

There is an increased understanding and empathy with others which reduces the friction caused by great contrast. Feelings of

Horse Chestnut

intolerance and impatience can be lessened. Horse chestnut creates a flow between differing energies-rather than agitation. This releases emotional pressure from the Spleen and Bladder meridians.

Base, solar plexus and crown chakra are affected. There is increased knowledge of what one requires and desires for physical well-being and balanced survival. There is a growth of wisdom that allows calm and clarity to develop and the ability to find one's personal space and life.

There is a regulation of energy flow between the crown and base chakras. This prevents any unnecessary build-up of energy and also grounds turbulence. This stress-free movement helps to bring about peace to agitated thoughts and repetitive patterns.

This calm and balance improves mental functioning. Fears, anxieties and over-rational intellectual or obsessive thought are lessened. Having quietened the surface levels of the mind the attention can dwell upon the deeper flows of intuition and the realisation that mind creates personal reality.

Signature: The white "candles" like a steady, calm mind, are undisturbed by emotional "winds".

Comment: Edward Bach used this tree essence, called White Chestnut, for internal, repetitive thoughts or anxieties. The bark, when dried by gentle heat, has tonic, narcotic and febrifuge properties and is used for intermittent fevers, given as an infusion. External ulcers have also been treated with the bark infusion. The fruits are effective as a treatment for haemorrhoids, rheumatism and neuralgia.

Italian Alder

Italian Alder
(Alnus cordata)

Key: PROTECTED PEACE; FOR DELICATE ENERGIES; COURAGE; GUILT; POOR SELF-WORTH; HEALING EMOTIONAL HURTS; PINK.

The Italian alder, originating from Corsica and southern Italy, is the largest member of that family. In the wild it grows in dense thickets on damp ground, but it is tolerant of dry soil and is now much planted in towns and roadsides. It grows rapidly, has a tall, domed shape with bright, dense foliage up to 80 feet (24 metres). The leaves are heart-shaped, the catkins much fatter and larger than the native alder and the cones are heavier and more elongated.

This tree brings peace, love and protection for delicate energies. It can be helpful when there is either shyness or over-aggression. It provides courage and healing where new beginnings are needed.

Italian alder balances the Governor and Heart meridians to strengthen self-esteem and the feeling of being supported. Thus, it is for those who feel useless, unworthy, not valued, lacking in support, and so on. The soul body is also cleared of imbalances caused by guilt and this too, increases feelings of self-worth restoring energy to the physical being.

Peace and quiet enters the emotions restoring balance to the individual and the surroundings. It is able to heal emotional hurts and feelings of unworthiness and of being unloved.

At the finest levels of function Italian alder allows deep healing energies to enter from other dimensions. These are powerful protective levels of awareness that can neutralise polluting and aggressive vibrations.

Signature: The abundant upward growth and heart-shaped leaves.

Comment: Such an energy established in urban environments does much both at the physical and at subtle levels to cleanse the atmosphere. It is interesting to note that this tree has only begun to be planted in the last thirty years or so in Britain.

Ivy
(Hedera helix)

Key: FEAR; ANXIETY; HIDDEN FEARS; HEART CHAKRA; GUIDE AND PROTECTOR; GREEN-YELLOW.

The ivy is one of the few plants that can thrive in deep shade. It can only very rarely be called a tree in its own right, though some old stems are as thick as tree trunks. Ivy is a climber, using walls and other plants for support as it reaches for height and sunlight. The triangular and five-pointed leaves are evergreen and often cover the floor of woods and copses. Ivy bears clusters of yellow flowers late in October, almost the last food for many insects. The black berries ripen over the next year.

As an essence ivy is very specific in its actions. Anxiety is the state it helps to resolve. Ivy specifically works with the chakra points at the wrists that help to ease hidden fears. Placing a few drops on these points will immediately reduce stress levels.

The heart chakra and its subtle channels, the nadis, are also strengthened bringing an increased calm and focus, as well as a greater sensitivity to one's surroundings. There is an increased ability to face fears and clearly examine those strong feelings for the underlying causes. Ivy helps to rationally identify emotions and needs. By acting in this way stress is released and immune system function improves.

Ivy is an essential guide and protector both in working with tree spirits and confronting one's own inner fears successfully.

Signature: Lives in both dark and light. It flowers once it reaches the sunlight.

Ivy

Juᴅas Tʀee
(Cercis siliquastrum)

Key: CHANNELLING; ORIGINAL THOUGHT; NEW IDEAS; OPENNESS; SOOTHING; THROAT CHAKRA; DISCERNMENT; BLUE - INDIGO.

Judas tree is native to dry, rocky places in western Asia and southeastern Europe. The name probably derives from "Judaea Tree" in which area it is particularly common. Judas tree is a small, broad, spreading tree up to 33 ft. (10m). The leaves are kidney-shaped and before they fully emerge the flowers appear around the end of May. The flowers are bright magenta-pink and grow singly and in bunches straight from the bark of twigs and trunk. It only really flourishes in the warmer parts of Britain, in sheltered spots.

As an essence Judas tree enables completely original thought, as if springing from nowhere. The seeds of new ideas arise from the deepest levels of the mind, where all available information has been stored and explored.

There is an openness and willingness to listen to one's own feelings. This can break patterns of repeating behaviour to do with past regrets, enabling a new view of life. The Lung meridian is strengthened.

Communication and expression of personal opinion can be more direct, forceful and of a more practical nature. Nonetheless the essence also calms and soothes turbulent, passionate and angry states and enables rational, cool consideration of any situation involving the emotions. Throat chakra blocks are helped to clear in this way.

163

Judas Tree

The development of channelling abilities is enhanced, together with the discrimination to discern the truthfulness within such thoughts.

Signature: The deep pink-magenta flowers (the colour of inspiration, universal energy and unity) spring straight from the bare bark.

Laburnum

Labuꞧnum

(Laburnum x watereri "Vossi")
(Laburnum anagyroides)

Key: DETOXICATION; RELEASE OF SHOCK AND TRAUMA; GROWTH OF CREATIVE POTENTIAL; OPTIMISM; POSITIVITY; LETTING GO; ORANGE-GOLD.

Laburnum is native to the hill regions of central Europe. It is a small tree up to 30ft (9m) with smooth, olive green- brown bark and a tendency to arch. In early summer yellow, pea-like flowers appear in long, pendulous strings. These ripen into green pods containing highly poisonous, shiny black seeds. Laburnum was first grown in Britain in 1595 and has been widely planted as an ornamental tree. The wood is hard, easy to work, finishes well and has long been used in cabinet-making.

The natural hybrid, Voss's Laburnum, arose in 1856 in the Tyrol and later (1865) also in Surrey, from *L. anagyroides* and *L. alpinum*. It is this variety that is most commonly planted for its spectacular flowers.

Laburnum creates the space and opportunity in which to allow the release of underlying imbalances, shock and traumas. By doing so it allows a growth of creative potential. There is a relaxation of muscular and nervous tension as the mental body is balanced and rigid belief systems or inappropriate concepts are abandoned. This allows a rapid detoxification of the system to take place. Likewise there is an increase in optimism, positivity and discrimination.

The throat chakra is stimulated and relaxation in this area will release tension, increase the ability to communicate and understand lessons, and listen to what is of use to the body systems - both physical and other forms of nutrition.

167

The release of long-held stress memories brings a new balance and lightness to the emotions.

Signature: The fountain of yellow flowers and the somewhat weeping shape of the tree suggests letting go and the release of long held stresses. The dark seeds can be seen as the poisons released from the deep levels of the self. The heartwood is black and ebony-like whilst the sapwood is yellow - the darkness of the inner is changed to the joy of the outer.

Comment: Laburnum is an extremely graceful and beautiful little tree. However all parts and particularly the black seeds are extremely toxic causing sleepiness, convulsions, coma and death. Particular care needs to be taken when working with this spirit.

LaRch
(Larix decidua)

Key: WILL TO EXPRESS; WISDOM AND AWARENESS; EXPLORATION; ARTISTIC ACTIVITY; BLUE-ORANGE.

Larch is the only deciduous conifer native to Europe. It is a mountain tree suited to long winters and short growing periods. Larch has a straight, single, tapering trunk with long down-swung branches that make a narrow conical crown. It is fast growing yet can live for as long as 700 years. Female flowers are bright red and ripen into small cones that stay on the tree for many years. The male flowers are yellow and bud-like. Larch was introduced as an ornamental tree in Britain as early as 1629 but it was during the 18th and 19th centuries especially that it was planted as a timber tree in huge numbers. Hybrid and Japanese larches are also planted where conditions favour them.

Larch helps to achieve balance through understanding the power of communication and the power of silence. It encourages wise judgement. In fact, larch introduces wisdom and awareness at every level so that it links to the creative, organising energies of the universe.

The main energies of this tree focus on the balance and expression of complementary energies particularly associated with the functions of the throat and sacral chakras, which can be characterised by the will to express the self and the desire to experience the outside of self.

The sacral chakra is affected, which controls and directs the physical energy towards expression and exploration of other beings in relationships. It motivates the joy for life and activates healing creativity.

Larch

Larch is an excellent essence for artistic activity bringing in both inspiration and the means to carry ideas into the world.

As a healer, larch can bring soothing and cooling energy to quite deep levels of hurt. There is greater acceptance of the physical levels of existence and the ability to let go and dissolve issues and experiences from the past.

Signature: Its fast straight growth and ability to let go (shed its leaves). The golden autumn colouring of orange-gold, signifies creativity and wisdom.

Comment: Edward Bach used larch for those who felt they lacked the energy to succeed. Larch is an easily recognisable tree, often appearing untidy, unwell or even dying. But it knows what it is doing and is quite a friendly, very resinous, tree.

Lawson Cypress

172

Lawson Cypress
(Chamaecyparus lawsoniana)

Key: THE PATH; REALISTIC PLANS; RECOGNITION OF REQUIRED ACTION; APPROPRIATE CHANGE; INTERNAL CLARITY; DETERMINATION; TURQUOISE.

Lawson cypress has a very small natural range along 150 miles of N.W.Pacific coastal America between North California and Oregon. It forms groups within the redwood forest. The buttressed trunk with thick reddish-brown fibrous bark reaches up to 200 feet or more. When in the open branches grow right from ground level. Lawson cypress was introduced into Britain in 1854 when seeds were sent to Lawson's nursery in Edinburgh. Some of these first trees are now over 100 feet. Although its form remains stable in the wild, once introduced into Europe it produced over 70 cultivars. It comes from a mild climate yet is very hardy, though subject to wind burn. Lawson cypress flowers in spring. At the end of the branches male and female reddish bud-shaped flowers appear. These rapidly ripen to form small cones. When seed falls it lies dormant for about five years, begins slow growth for another two, then can grow up to 10 inches a year. The wood is white, soft and even-grained with a ginger-like scent.

Lawson cypress activates those areas that are needed to identify correct action or the most appropriate direction in which to move. It brings energy into the base, sacral, solar plexus and brow chakras. In the base chakra it stimulates the required activity and discipline. The sacral chakra brings in the willingness to fulfil desires and to be flexible and creative in achieving them. The solar plexus is more closely linked to the energies of the higher self so that the individual's true needs can be communicated through intuition, dream and other symbolic forms. The essence also helps to clear out nonrealistic, deluded or fantasised futures. The brow chakra maintains the overview and is enabled to clearly define in terms of thought, the "feelings" activated in the lower chakras. All the subtle channels associated with these chakras are also cleared and activated.

In this way Lawson cypress helps to bring the recognition of required actions; initiates change if that is appropriate; allows internal communication at the physical body-intelligence level; allows greater internal clarity to determine ones real needs, rather than those based wholly on intellect or fads.

Signature: This tree maintains itself discretely in its own space but when given the opportunity of circumstance will show great flexibility and adaptation of form, colour and size in its cultivars. It grows to a great height and yet bears branches up the trunk from its lowest levels - evenness, balance, determination.

Comment: Because of its architectural form and fast growth Lawson cypress has become a very popular landscaping tree in gardens. Unfortunately many forget it is essentially a forest tree and become antagonistic to it when it begins to dominate the inadequate space it has been given.

This is a potent, powerful spirit. Learn to link with it and listen to it. Disdain and dismissiveness is wholly inappropriate - particularly where the tree relies on mankind to place it in our environment. We sully our own souls by these ignorant, casual value judgements.

Leyland Cypress
(x Cupressocyparis leylandii)

Key: FREEDOM; EXPANSION; COMPOSURE; TOLERANCE; HUMOUR; SOLITUDE; GREEN.

This tree is a natural cross between the Nootka cypress fertilised by a Monterey cypress, which happened in Welshpool in 1888. In some respects, therefore, this is a truly native species, having its genesis in Wales! Leyland cypress quickly became popular as a hedging plant, combining the rapid growth of the Monterey and the hardiness of the Nootka. The trunk has numerous short branches from base to crown, both usually invisible through the thick, evergreen foliage. Small yellow male flowers appear in spring at the branch-tips. Female flowers are green and ripen later into small, green cones.

There is a sense of expansiveness and freedom. Where there has been anxiety and worry regarding the future, and where there is a lack of confidence and faith in positive outcomes, this essence re-energises the Spleen meridian to regain composure and trust.

It is possible to let go of unreal possibilities and delusions. A more stable and positive attitude is created with forgiveness, tolerance and compassion for oneself grows, together with an increased sense of humour.

All this creates a sense of freedom and a space that feels comfortable. It helps to clear the head and shakes off muzziness. A useful essence for those who are frightened of being on their own or who are uncomfortable in their own company.

Leyland Cypress

Signature: The structure of trunk and branches are kept hidden. The tree is planted as a fast-growing screen against noise, wind and to maintain privacy. Establishing personal boundaries. Both parent trees grow on the Pacific coast of America in spacious, wild surroundings.

Comment: It is interesting to note that this spontaneous generation of a new species occurred between two different, unrelated genera of tree at a time when the Victorian Age was fully occupied with the exploration of the "green" energies of freedom, boundaries, discipline and power at the level of the individual, the society and the nation. 1888 was also the year Mme. Blavatsky published *"Isis Unveiled"*.

It is well worth getting to know this tree in its natural form if possible. We are so used to seeing it only as a square-cut wall of feathery green that it is easy to forget that Leyland cypress is a magnificent tree in its own right.

All the cypresses have potent scents of great variety, some peppery, some sweet and so on. Next time you pass a leylandii hedge take a deep breath in and acknowledge the spirit presence - just because something is common and useful there is no need to ignore it.

Lilac

Lílac
(Syringa vulgaris)

Key: SPINE; POSTURE; FLEXIBILITY; SEVEN CHAKRAS; NATURE SPIRITS; INTEGRATION OF ENERGY SYSTEMS AND ENVIRONMENT; VIOLET.

Lilac was introduced to Britain in 1621 by John Tradescant, a prolific gardener of the time, from its native habitats of eastern Europe and Asia Minor. It now grows wild in many parts of the country. Lilac blossoms around May in large multi-flowered, strongly scented spikes of white, cream, lilac and purple. Lilac rarely grows tall, though it can reach 25ft (7.5m) and is usually a many-stemmed shrub with large, heart shaped leaves and a fibrous peeling bark.

The lilac essence mainly influences the spinal column. It works immediately on this area and so it is useful before any spinal adjustment, helping to stabilise any corrections, by increasing the energy flowing through the spinal channels and relaxing the supporting muscles. Lilac helps to correct posture and flexibility in the spine, largely through its influence on the subtle channels and major seven spinal chakras.

Because of the central role of the spine, both physically and at subtle anatomical levels, lilac can be a useful adjunct to many corrective and evolutionary procedures. It will help restore balance throughout the system and may be indicated in instances where there is no apparent involvement of back or spine.

The lilac plant itself is thought to have a close link to many forms of nature spirits who use the energy of the lilac to elevate their own levels of awareness. This essence can also, then, be used to help us to attune more closely with these realms of awareness, both through the supportive energy link and also because lilac realigns so many fundamental energy systems within the body consciousness.

Signature: The heartwood of lilac is violet, reflecting the healing potential upon the spine and central energy channels. The sweet scented, small but substantial flowers cluster together and align into a tall spike, echoing the energy channels and centres of the body becoming integrated together.

Lime

(Tilea x europa; Tilea platyphyllos; Tilea cordata)

Key: DEVELOPMENT; CALMING AND SUPPORTING; EXTREMES OF EMOTION; CHANGE; GROWTH OF AWARENESS; LIGHTNESS AND JOY; GREEN-YELLOW.

The common lime is thought to be a cross between two other native species, the small-and large-leaved limes. It is a tall tree that begins branching near the ground making a tall domed crown up to 130 ft (40m). The large-leaved lime can be distinguished by the fact that it doesn't sprout from the base, unlike all other types. It reaches 100ft.(30m) and has ascending branches around a narrow domed crown. The small-leaved lime has downward arching branches and, unlike the large-leaved lime, the leaf stalks are not hairy. Both have heart-shaped leaves, while in common lime the leaf bases are almost straight. All produce creamy clusters of sweet scented flowers in June and July. The order of flowering is: large-leaved limes followed by the common and small-leaved limes.

Limes are long-lived trees, some of the oldest trees in Britain, and were one of the main woodland species. The soft wood is sweet scented and easily worked, the flowers are calming and relaxing, the inner bark is fibrous and can be woven into mats and rope.

At a physical level this tree essence is calming and supporting. The endocrine system is helped to regulate itself and there is an enlivening of life-force at the cellular levels.

Lime calms anxieties within the mind and helps to ease extremes of emotion, particularly when these are to do with making practical use of one's own developmental potential.

Lime

Often the suppression of natural skills seriously depletes our life-energy or directs the energy into negative, damaging behaviour patterns. The Gall Bladder meridian is helped to restore a positive balance to these strong emotions.

The solar plexus chakra and the eighth chakra, located above the head, are brought into action. This introduces the creative power necessary to move from one level of activity to another-whether that is a new awareness or a change of life-focus-in such a way that individual balance and the structure of the personality is maintained. Lime is thus useful in times of rapid growth or change. It can be of great benefit to those who are unable or unwilling to accept or use their higher faculties and subtle sensing skills. Doubts and fears of all sorts ease, and the familiar entrenched patterns of past behaviour are easier to overcome.

Signature: A tree that can live for many centuries, grows to a very large size and yet constantly is able to offer itself as food from leaf, fruit and flower to a great number of insects, birds and animals. The heart-shaped leaves.

Comment: The lime is also known as the linden, its Germanic name. On the Continent the tree is still often found at the heart of the village as guardian and focus for the community. As a native tree, lime never naturally extended into northern Britain or Ireland and its apparent omission from Celtic tree lore, such as ogham lists, suggests an Irish origin for such material. In mainland Britain lime would have been such a predominant woodland species and so extremely useful both medicinally and as a material resource that there is no reason, other than especial sanctity, why it would not have been included along with other tree species. Lime essence is a very light, refreshing joyous energy: very good to infuse into a heavy atmosphere.

Lucombe Oak

Lucombe Oak
(Quercus hispanica "Lucombeana")

Key: CREATIVE ENERGY; INSPIRATION; IDEAS; KINDNESS; LEARNING FROM EXPERIENCE; CREATIVE INTELLIGENCE; SACRAL CHAKRA; ORANGE-VIOLET.

Lucombe oak is named after an Exeter nurseryman who found a natural cross between turkey oak and cork oak. When the two original hybrids produced acorns in 1792 they were grown and distributed. There are many forms but the common Lucombe oak is fully evergreen with shiny dark green leaves and pointed teeth and has a slightly corky bark with keel-like swellings on the trunk near the branches. Other types are closer to one parent or the other with lighter, thick corky bark or not fully evergreen. It can be found in parks and gardens throughout Britain but is most common in Devon, especially in Exeter itself. Like other oaks it produces clusters of yellow, male catkins in spring and female flowers that ripen into acorns enclosed in a mossy green cup during the second year.

The focus of this tree is a life-supporting creativity bringing inspiration and ideas.

The crown chakra is able to infuse the mind with the awareness of evolutionary activity. The mental body is thus energised and is enabled to act with a greater commitment for change and growth. Any state of lethargy, lack of commitment or confusion can be helped with Lucombe oak.

There is increased tolerance and kindness born of wisdom and compassion. Stressful and life-harming beliefs are released by an infusion of non-aggressive awareness. This can be deeply healing.

Individual consciousness, encapsulated within the fourth, or astral, body is helped to remove fears relating to personality, past lives and life-purpose. There is a clarity of mind with a greater ability to focus and learn from experience.

At its subtlest Lucombe oak reveals the finest levels of inspiration, where creativity and creative intelligence spring from the unmanifest, absolute nature of reality. With this quality of energy accessible the full potential can be brought forward in a dynamic and energetic manner before it becomes diluted and constrained by limitations.

Lucombe oak embodies creativity, creative intelligence and manifestation of the creative urge.

Comment: Like all oaks, Lucombe oak focuses itself on creating and holding energy in a form where it can manifest in physical reality. Creativity at all levels is suggested - both reproductive, intellectual and artistic. It can be one of the primary energies for bringing dynamic clarity to the functions of the second chakra.

Magnolia
(Magnolia x soulangeana)

Key: RESTLESSNESS; RELEASING FEARS; VULNER-
ABILITY; HEART CHAKRA; HAPPINESS; OPEN AND
RELAXED; GREEN.

An open-branched, short-trunked tree growing to 25 ft,
magnolia is well-loved for its flowers during April and May. As
buds they resemble steady white candle flames and as flowers
they bear a similarity to lotuses or pink and white doves
alighting on the branches.

Magnolia is a large family with members native to North
America and China where different species have been used
medicinally for protection against malaria to lowering of blood
pressure. This common variety is a cross between two Chinese
species grown near Paris in the 19th century.

Magnolia helps with the understanding of the healing process,
releasing fears to increase calm and the inherent healing
potential within the self.

Stomach and Governor meridians become activated to remove
feelings of vulnerability and lack of clarity. Helps where there is
an unsettling restlessness in which nothing satisfies.

The heart chakra and its nadis are cleansed of stress and
trauma allowing a greater freedom of emotional expression and
relaxation. The crown chakra is enabled to clarify true identity
and the validity of past and present experiences. This has a
strengthening effect on the immune system, which, after all,
represents personal identity at a cellular and chemical level.

Magnolia

When there are major life-decisions to be made and a need to clarify direction and what should be done, the causal subtle body, the fine level of awareness that patterns how we are, is energised. This helps when there are difficult choices. Heart and mind are brought into equilibrium and this allows calm and happiness in which to make the correct decisions.

Signature: The open, relaxed growth; the flowers resemble the subtle colours of the lotus, and so therefore the chakras.

Manna Ash

Manna Ash
(Fraxinus ornus)

Key: HAPPY WITH ONESELF; HEALING EMOTIONS; OPENNESS AND HONESTY; PURIFICATION AND INTEGRATION; COMFORT; NOURISHING; PINK.

The manna ash was introduced into Britain in 1700, though it is usually grown as a graft on the common ash. It is native in Asia and southern Europe. It is a small, round-crowned tree growing to 80ft (24m). The leaves are densely packed and of similar form to common ash though shorter and less pointed. It is the flowers of manna ash that are its most noticeable feature, starting off as bright green clustered buds that open in May or June as creamy-white scented flowers, elongating into masses of feathery threads.

Manna ash works primarily with healing the emotions. It helps to bring the recognition of what is needed to establish peace. It also allows an openness and honesty regarding one's true nature and what are the main motivating desires. This in itself can release deep blocks to self-expression.

Seeing more clearly one's true nature and being honest with oneself increases the energy available throughout the entire meridian system. The Governing meridian is strengthened. The Heart meridian is also given energy to clear emotional blocks from the heart. Manna ash increases self-worth and allows a process of self-acceptance to bring purification and trans-formation. Manna ash helps to sort out unresolved issues. It will also help to integrate the subtle bodies and this reduces aggravation and destructive tendencies caused by conflicts of emotion. Relationships of all kinds are seen in a wider and more constructive perspective.

The healing of subtle body imbalances and disturbances leads to an easing of mental stress. A quiet, creative level of consciousness is more easily accessed from which to draw greater healing.

At its finest levels manna ash allows a flow of wisdom and healing creativity from the level of pure consciousness, the source of all.

Signature: Mistakenly thought to be the source of manna that sustained the tribes of Israel in the desert, manna ash, although not a desert-dwelling tree, still comforts and feeds us at an emotional level.

Medlar

(Mespilus germanicus)

Key: BOUNDLESS; "RAISON D'ETRE"; CORE STRENGTHS; SECURE EXPANSIVENESS; STRENGTH; HUMOUR; BRIGHTNESS; CONFIDENCE; INTERNAL SWEETNESS; RED-GOLD.

A small, gnarled tree to 20ft originally from the Caucasus. Its fruit was popular with Greeks and Romans, the latter introducing the medlar into Britain. The leaves are large and downy with a single white wild rose-like flower at the end of each twig in summer. The scent is strong and not entirely pleasant. Medlar fruit is unusual - it doesn't fall from the tree and is only edible when it is over-ripe - very often after a few frosts or having been picked for a few weeks. Both flower and fruit are unmistakable.

Medlar essence energises personal core patterns, one's "raison d'etre", and helps them to develop into physical and practical expression. Increased motivation, enthusiasm and drive with a feeling of boundless energy to achieve goals.

The sacral and solar plexus chakras are strengthened. There is an increase in joy and happiness, and a deep "gut feeling" of safety and security. Creativity and the finest levels of self-awareness are more easily grounded into the practical desire to manifest and make real. Personal needs and neuroses are put into a broader context of the underlying enfoldment of the universal energies. Small selfishness is tempered by a feeling of secure expansiveness.

There is an expansion of strength, humour, brightness and creative intelligence that affects both the emotions and the spirituality.

193

Medlar

Signature: The fruits remain attached to the tree: security, confidence. Adverse conditions only serve to "blet" or ripen, the internal sweetness.

Mimosa

Mímosa
(Acacia dealbata)

Key: SENSITIVITY; INFORMATION FLOW; SMOOTHNESS; IDENTIFICATION; EXPRESSION; YELLOW.

Also known as the silver wattle, this tree originally comes from S. E. Australia and Tasmania where it grows in mountain gullies and on the banks of streams. It is quite widely planted in southern Europe but cannot survive cold winters or exposed conditions. The mild climate in the South West of England means that it is quite a common sight to see the small, bright yellow, fragrant clusters of flowers in January and February, just after the evergreen blue-green feathery leaves begin a new growth. Mimosa can grow to 65ft. The yellow pom-pom like flowers are often used in flower arranging.

Mimosa increases the sensitivity of the nervous system to internal body stimuli. This helps to improve the flow of energy and information between different systems, encouraging a smoother functioning.

The essence affects the Small Intestine meridian and the Large Intestine meridians, particularly with those issues to do with the assimilation of food at a physical level, as well as ideas and information at a mental level and the ability, at whatever level, to let go and release what is not required. This can be of benefit in any cleansing or detoxifying process.

There is a beneficial effect on the emotions, with an increased sense of peace.

A minor chakra in the upper throat is stimulated and this gives the will to express one's thoughts and to speak up.

The mental body is better balanced so that greater information and clarification can be received from the intuition. The subtle, causal body is steered more towards self-motivation and the power to express one's universal nature in an individual way.

Signature: The delicate leaves and globe-like clusters of flowers. Yellow: clarity, mental organisation, identification processes.

Midland Hawthorn
(Crataegus laevigata)

Key: EXPANSION; EMOTIONAL PEACE; HEART CENTRE; INTEGRATED SPIRITUALITY; ENERGY AND ENTHUSIASM FOR LIFE; CURIOSITY; INNOVATION; GREEN-RED.

A less common variety of hawthorn in the wild, though more widely planted in gardens for its blossom, the midland hawthorn grows on heavier soils. It can be identified by a more fluted, twisted trunk and has leaves that are more rounded and less indented then common hawthorn. Although its flowers can be white, the varieties chosen for planting are pink or deep red. "Paul's Scarlet" is the richest of reds with double petalled flowers.

The essence brings the quality of spaciousness and deep peace to relationship issues. The small selfish viewpoint is broadened out and relaxed to allow a calm overview.

Much energy focuses around the heart and its subtle centres, especially those to do with directing the heart energy into spiritual growth. The temptation to over-emotionalise and "go overboard" on spiritual quests is balanced so that spiritual aspects can become integrated into everyday life.

There is an increased desire to live life to the full, to enjoy, learn, use and discover as much of life as is humanly possible. This extra energy is an antidote for the weak-willed or those who fear exploration, and yet helps to moderate reckless or impulsive tendencies. With this enthusiasm to grow and investigate for oneself there comes an awareness of innovative concepts and inspirations which allow for personal expansion.

Midland Hawthorn

Signature: The rich red blossom energises the senses at a time of year when all life is expanding and growing into summer.

Comment: Like many other species, the hawthorns seem to focus their group energy on a similar area of life. Here it is primarily the heart and aspects of relationship, growth, personal freedom and expansion that can be seen in hawthorn, Glastonbury thorn and Midland hawthorn.

Monkey Puzzle Tree

Monkey Puzzle Tree
(Araucacia araucana)

Key: FIERCE COMPASSION; GROUNDING; PROTECTING; CYCLES OF TIME; CONTINUITY OF AWARENESS; TALKING TO THE LONG MEMORY OF THE PLANET; PINK-RED.

The Chile pine, known throughout Britain by its Victorian name the "monkey puzzle tree", is native to a small area around the Andean mountain, Volcan Llaima. Its name derives from the Araucanian peoples who depend quite heavily on the large seeds as a food source. Five seedlings were brought back to Kew Gardens in 1795 by botanist Alexander Menzies who had never seen a specimen in the wild. In 1884 more seeds were brought from Chile and the major plantings took place then. The tree is unmistakable with each branch completely covered in overlapping, dark green, rigid leaves. Male and female flowers appear on separate trees, the fertilised cone ripening over three years. The monkey puzzle can grow to 80ft (24m) and has a neat, domed crown often losing its lower branches. It is fairly short-lived, averaging 100 years.

The monkey puzzle tree is characterised by action that is expressed through caring, understanding and compassion. It will calm aggression but still allows that energy to be manifested in a creative, forceful way. The essence is strongly energising, earthing and protecting from negativity.

One particular characteristic of this tree is that it enables a great understanding and the experience of joyfulness in witnessing the continuous cycles of change upon the planet - sunrise to sunset, day and night, heat and cold, summer and winter, activity and stillness. The perception of the underlying stability and continuity of awareness running throughout, expands the sense of time and space. This enlarged view helps the release of tension and anxiety. Talking to the long memory of the planet, and becoming enfolded within the story.

Signature: The way each leaf overlaps from the last suggests the overlapping and continuous cycles of growth and time. The nuts were the main sustaining food crop of the Araucanian people: a fierce tree providing plentiful harvests.

Comment: In Britain the monkey-puzzle is synonymous with Victorian park and garden planning, and with that period's rather fusty provincialism. It takes a fresh vision to go beyond this accreted, received view to see the tree in the context of its own energy.

Monterey Pine
(Pinus radiata)

Key: CONNECTEDNESS; REMOVAL OF DEEP STRESSES; PHYSICAL CONFIDENCE; BROW CHAKRA; ARTISTIC CREATIVITY; VIOLET-RED.

During the Ice Age, pines grew in the southern parts of North America. When the ice melted, a few small pockets remained only on the Monterey peninsula in California where it is a low-growing, wind-blown tree. Monterey pine was introduced to Britain in 1833. Here it grows rapidly. With dense triple needles of grass green and the ability to thrive in salt and windy exposed locations at low altitudes, it quickly became established as a windbreak.

In Britain the tree can grow twice as fast as normal, sometimes throughout the whole year, and has reached a height of over 180ft. In spring male flowers are found in long spikes at the base of new shoots, heavy with yellow pollen. Female flowers are red-brown and found at the tops of new shoots. The ripened cones can remain on the tree for up to 30 years.

Monterey pine helps the removal of deep stresses from the system - particularly those relating to speaking out against perceived injustices and the failure to speak out when necessary. It becomes easier to be happy in one's own company and self-sufficient.

There is an increasing sense of purpose and ease with the self and the surroundings. A calm and clarity reaches the emotions.

There is a sense of physical well-being - getting in touch with the body. There is an increased confidence in the physical body.

Monterey Pine

Subtle perceptive abilities are enhanced with the possibility of past-life information and an increased understanding of ideas, concepts and other energy planes.

The release of deep-seated stresses helps to promote self-expression and artistic creativity, so this essence can be useful when there are artistic blocks. The new flow of energy brings a sense of deep peace and connectedness to everything. There is a balance between active and passive modes of behaviour, between aggression and submission and between male and female polarities.

With increased self-expression there is a release of pressure from the solar plexus and gut areas. This extra confidence relaxes preconceptions and rigidity of beliefs and so allows clearer evaluation of the importance and relevance of any information and thought patterns emerging from the deep mind.

Signature: The ability to survive and thrive in many different conditions. The clouds of yellow pollen: relaxation, generosity, fecundity. Fast growth and retention of cones: security, control, confidence.

Comment: Pines are quite difficult to distinguish from each other-particularly when young. Look out for the bright green needles of Monterey pine in groups of three, and the very dense foliage. Pine is known to activate the brow chakra and subtle energy channels. Gurudas suggests the following: take the essence and meditate with eyes closed on something known to have an auric field, allowing your imagination to stimulate the brow chakra. Visualise a clear and beautiful blue eye in the centre of the forehead opening up to look around.

Essence or resin can be rubbed on the centre of the forehead to help balance its activation. This can be augmented with frankincense and myrrh, which have similar effects.

Mulberry

Mulberry
(Black Mulberry) (Morus nigra)

Key: WRATH; DETACHMENT FROM THE SOURCE OF PAIN; CYNICS AND CRITICS; CONSTRUCTIVE ENERGY OF ANGER; OVERSEEING LOVE; DEEP RED-MAGENTA.

A smallish, gnarled, rough looking tree with large heart-shaped leaves. In May it produces green male and female catkins, the latter which ripen into large, rich red fruit. Perhaps originating from the Middle East, mulberry was brought west by the Greeks and Romans. It has been grown in Britain since 1550. The Chinese variety is white mulberry upon which silkworms feed. Both species have medicinal properties: the leaves are used for colds, 'flu, eye infections and nosebleeds; the branches for rheumatic pain and hypertension; the root bark for coughs, asthma and bronchitis; the fruit for tinnitus and greying of hair.

Here there is emotional healing. Mulberry brings compassion, peace and a necessary detachment from the source of pain.

It works through the Spleen, Liver and Circulation-sex (Pericardium) meridians. It can be for those who decry any views that differ from their own and who will not see deeper truths, and for those who are jaded and cynical about the world - dominant, worldly-wise cynics.

For those attached to a painful situation or event and carry within them great remorse, Mulberry helps to heal the energy link and brings peace. There is freedom from past pain and remorse.

It changes the energy of anger towards more constructive ends where it can be mastered and fully expressed through understanding the truth of the underlying situation. It will allow full expression of feelings but helps to curb excessive wrathfulness.

The chakra at the solar plexus is activated to protect fine levels of emerging awareness and to manifest these in practical ways.

The mind is given a degree of energy that enables inspirational concepts and ideas to find creative expression - particularly when the ideas seem to be coming from beyond personal experience.

On a universal level this essence acts as a pathway to some of the superphysical consciousnesses of the solar system, the loving intelligence that directs and oversees the creative processes in each area of the physical cosmos.

Signature: The rough bark and rough leaves in contrast to the heart-shaped leaves and substantial, rich, sweet fruit (that only become properly edible once the tree is well grown).

Norway Maple
(Acer platanoides)

Key: HEALING LOVE; HAPPINESS; TAKING BACK CONTROL; RELAXATION OF TENSION; EMPOWERMENT; ENLIVENING; PINK-GOLD.

Norway maple is a native in Europe apart from Britain and the Lowlands. It is a large deciduous tree with a short bole and a wide-domed crown reaching to 90ft. Bright green leaves are typically maple shaped and turn bright yellow in autumn. In spring, before the leaves, it produces a profusion of surprisingly bright yellow-green flowers in erect bunches. Introduced into Britain in 1683 Norway maple is now very common and easily self-seeds in sandy soil. It is also popular as a town tree, partly because of its rapid growth when young.

Primarily healing on emotional levels, this essence brings love, acceptance, healing and nurturing energy to states of emotional shock and trauma.

The Triple-Warmer and Liver meridians are cleansed to restore a sense of lightness and happiness.

The crown chakra is able to access healing and creative energy, and this flows down into the body to enable one to take back control of situations where there is a feeling of powerlessness. There is clarity in accepting the reality of circumstances and finding ways to work within them.

The emotional and spiritual bodies are aligned and this will help the most subtle aspirations of the personality guide the feeling level towards appropriate activity and direction.

Norway Maple

There is an increased understanding of situations and this encourages relaxation and particularly release of tension at the solar plexus. Fears and anxiety ease, joy and comfort increase.

As this process of relaxation and empowerment continues it is more possible to access deeper levels of personal potential where it is brought to awareness through inspiration and imagination. There is an ability to harmonise with universal qualities of compassion and healing, aligning to a creative flow of energy that creates freedom and healing.

Signature: The bright, fresh coloured blossoms in early spring indicate an enlivening of the qualities of the solar plexus and heart chakras.

Oak

Oak
(Quercus robur, Quercus petraea)

Key: MANIFESTATION; BRING FORTH AND BALANCE;
REALITY ANCHOR; MOTIVATION; ORIGINS OF PRIMAL
ENERGY; GROWTH; RED

The two native oaks in Britain can be identified by form and
habitat, where they haven't cross-bred many times. The
common oak, also called the English oak or pedunculate oak,
favours lower land and heavier soils. It sends out large,
horizontal branches from a comparatively short, squat trunk. It
is the host to the largest number of insects, lichen, birds and
animals of any native tree. The long tap-root makes it drought
resistant.

The sessile oak prefers wetter climates and lighter soils. Its
taller trunk and more compact shape is commonly seen in the
north, west and other upland regions. The common oak has
leaves with no stalks but acorns with stalks, whilst the sessile
oak has leaves with long stalks and acorns with none.

Oak flowers as it opens its leaves. The male catkins are yellow
green and cluster together soon becoming long, like knotted
strings. The female flowers are small buds at the branch ends,
green with bright red anthers. The English oak can reach
115ft(35m) and the sessile oak grows to 130ft (40m).

The energy of the oaks in general has to do with the ability to
manifest, to bring forth, maintain and balance reality. Steady
growth and drawing out potential from where it is hidden from
sight can be accomplished with oak.

The Heart meridian is brought into balance, which relaxes and
expands the emotions.

Many of the more subtle energy centres and channels of the body are given a boost of energy. For example, the eleventh chakra above the head is activated. This helps to integrate the personality located in time-space with the transpersonal collective, Higher self or soul group, making it easier to understand and direct the purpose of lifetime activities.

A minor chakra, not located in the physical body but in the aura, is strongly activated. It is located below the feet the same distance as the feet are from the base chakra. This is a dynamic anchor point both for the present moment, and into the Earth's own patterns. Security, belonging, taking one's place, stability, practicality, all rely on a firm grounding link that this chakra supplies. Keeping a body well and functioning requires the will to exist on this planet, here and now. Oak provides this motivation.

Oak essence doesn't specifically act on any one subtle body. It tends to give more energy to all bodies, though it doesn't realign them.

The spiritual state brought about by oak spirit is profoundly internalised, involuted and dwells at the unmanifest levels of creation. This undefined, non-dimensional area can seem threatening and empty - it is the Void - because it lacks the characteristic of boundaries, but it is in fact the vessel wherein all manifest creation is held. Once this vision is no longer reinterpreted in terms of its opposite (ie. Form), this Void becomes cognised and directly experienced as the origin of all possibilities, from which limitless expressions of the primal energy can be drawn.

Oak essence aids in the absorption and integration of these very deep, hidden energy levels from the primal sources of being. The oak spirit funnels it through the desire for growth and expansion into physical dimensions of reality, and will encourage delight in expressing the energy of growth in as many ways as possible.

At a practical level oak will give support to all forms of growth and expansion and will give stability where the polarities of existence are a little too apparent in one's life!

A calming, internalised energy will bring patience, new perspectives and a better grasp of the situation one is in.

Signature: The deep tap-root and the ability to sustain numerous other life-forms without detriment to itself.
The acorn and the cup: the form and void, absolute and relative states of existence.

Comment: The potential of exploration with this spirit is vast. Whilst working with the assessment the following phrases were caught: the void, the black/white hole; the means to manifest one from many; absorption within all possibilities and then revealing new patterns; communication with those hidden sources; to be held free of time, outside the flow; suspension beyond time; manifesting from nothing.

Edward Bach used only the female flowers of the English oak for those who carry on struggling and fighting against illness or adversity without loss of hope or effort.

The bark of oak has a strong astringent effect. It is also tonic and antiseptic. It can be used to reduce haemorrhaging and for diarrhoea and dysentery.

Oak galls, "oak apples", are created by the larvae of insects secreting a fluid that makes the plant cells develop abnormally. This then becomes the home and food of the insect until it matures and bores its way out. They are used in tanning, dying and making of inks. Galls are a powerful astringent, the most powerful of all vegetable sources, used as an internal tincture for dysentery, diarrhoea and cholera. The powder can be used to stop bleeding.

Osier

Osier

(Salix viminalis)

Key: SPIRITUAL VOID; ACCEPT AND LET GO; SOLAR PLEXUS CHAKRA; BALANCED RELATIONSHIPS; BROAD UNDERSTANDING; TOLERANCE.

The osier is a member of the willow family that is usually a many-stemmed shrub from 10 - 30ft (3-6m). It is regularly coppiced to create fast-growing shoots or "withies" used in basket weaving. It can be easily recognised in summer from its very long blade-like leaves, dark green on top and silvery undersides. The leaf edges are untoothed and rolled in slightly. The flowers are borne separately as "pussy willows".

This essence can be used when there is a need to accept and let go. It will relax the mind and let a deeper wisdom well up.

Osier strengthens the solar plexus chakra, particularly when it seems that a void lies behind existence and everything appears shallow and meaningless. This apparent blackness can be, in reality, an actual experience of the unrevealed, hidden or unmanifest levels of creation which has to be understood for what it is: the underlying vibration of all life.

Osier gives a more balanced approach to one's relationship with others, neither being too forceful, or overbearing, nor too willing to accept others' points of view. A broader understanding of concepts and experiences helps this approach. More energy can be given to personal beliefs so that it isn't felt necessary to indoctrinate others or to get your own way regardless of others' opinions.

At the mental level flexibility and creativity are encouraged in the concepts and ideas one holds and osier helps to acquire the wisdom enabling the individual to access and use the fundamental energy of the universe and the wisdom to use personal power correctly.

Signature: Being "cut down" is no disadvantage for the osier's vitality simply makes more rapid, more flexible and useful shoots. Lack becomes the means to expand.

Pear
(Pyrus communis)

Key: SERENITY; CALMS FEARS; CLEARS NERVOUS
SYSTEM; ZEST; DEEP PEACE.

The native pear, Pyrus cordata, is extremely rare existing only around the area of Plymouth, Devon, where it was identified as a separate species at the end of the last century. The common pear is most probably a naturalised tree originating from hybrids in southern Europe. It is often planted in gardens and parks as well as farmland and orchards. In winter pear is a dark, tall and sparsely branched tree resembling thorn in many ways. In April pear produces white flowers as the leaves emerge. Wild varieties sucker freely and produce small, very gritty fruit. Like apple it can be frequently found along roadsides and footpaths. The tree can reach 50ft. (15m).

Pear calms fears and brings clarity of mind, increasing the sense of peace and joy. It will help to clear and re-energise the nervous system after it has been blocked by the effects of past-life experiences or powerful belief systems. This encourages a sense of ease and relaxation throughout the nervous system, releasing physical tensions.

The Gall Bladder meridian is cleansed which increases the sense of serenity and happiness. There is a clarity, simplicity, confidence and inner calm: happy to be who one is.

The solar plexus chakra is involved increasing enthusiasm, activation and motivation for physical activity.

At its finest level pear brings a deep peace, an unimpeded flow of communication, a frictionless flow.

221

Pear

Persian Ironwood
(Parrotia persica)

Key: ALIENATION; SECURITY; GROUNDING; BELONGING TO EARTH; DEEPLY ENERGISING; ACTIVATION OF SELF-HEALING PROCESSES; SURVIVORS OF NATURAL DISASTERS; RED.

Persian ironwood is a small native tree of the Caucasus Mountains and northern Iran. It forms dense thickets of interlacing stems and branches, often fusing together. It can grow to 60 feet but usually only 25 feet in Britain. Persian ironwood is the only member of its genus, though it has features similar to the witch-hazel family. It flowers early in the year, usually January, producing dense clusters of red stamens upon the branches. It is planted as an ornamental for its plane-like bark, autumn foliage of golden-crimson red and the early show of flowers. When in leaf it can resemble a somewhat large-leaved beech, though it has a much greater density of branches. The wood is so hard as to be unworkable.

Persian ironwood is essentially grounding, earthing and energising in its functions. The essence increases the sense of security and emotional stability, especially when dealing with strong drives and emotions.

There is a greater recognition and understanding of one's intuitive faculties and, as a result, an increased sense of peace and joy as the mental functions become more integrated.

At an emotional level, the energising influence enables a greater expression of harmony, love and non-aggression. After all, negative emotions and reactions arise from fears that have their basis in self-doubt and insecurity. When one knows that one is invincible there can be no enemy and no fear.

Persian Ironwood

On very fine levels of energy this tree helps to link to the super-consciousness of the planetary energies as a whole. This is not quite the same as attunement to the earth as a planet, but more as if it were a link to the higher self, or the potential future self of Mother Earth. With this link there comes a strong sense of being connected, a new sense of self, and an influx of joy and happiness. It is as if we saw a glimpse of a future beyond our dreams, knew that we were a part of it and knew that we were totally, completely safe there.

On physical levels Persian ironwood may have a significant role in bringing subtle energies for change into the molecular structures of the cell. Certainly it is deeply energising and as such it will tend to activate self-healing processes. As the energies of Persian ironwood ground, as it were, the energies of the future into the present, were genetic changes likely to be of use to the individual, this essence might help initiate the process.

Signature: the convoluted, pipe-like branches, their inter-growth and the flowers sprouting straight from the branches.

Comment: Where there is chronic energy drain, such as in ME and with those who are too "open" to subtle vibrations causing emotional or physical imbalance, this tree works well. It has also been used to great effect to help those recovering from involvement in natural disasters, such as earthquakes. It helps re-establish confidence in the solidity of the planet.

Plane Tree

Plane Tree
(Platanus x acerifolia)

Key: FINE JUDGEMENT; CALM CLARITY; INTUITIVE
KNOWLEDGE; MELANCHOLICS; MEDITATIVE STATES;
BLUE-GOLD.

The Oriental plane (*Platanus orientalis*) is a massive tree that
can be many thousands of years old. It has a huge low bole that
sends out large branches that often rest upon the ground before
swinging upwards again. It was planted in Britain before 1600.
The commonest variety of plane seen is the London plane, a
hybrid between the oriental plane and American plane. Though
this is a familiar tree in towns and cities (hence its name)
because it survives pollution very well in poor soils, it is still a
large forest tree - the largest in Britain.

London plane probably arose in Tradescant's nursery in the
1650's where both parent trees are known to have existed. As
its Latin name suggests the leaves are similar in shape to the
sycamore, except generally larger and with a shiny surface. Of
the parents the oriental plane has deeply indented lobes and
the American plane, very shallow lobes. Male and female
flowers grow on the same tree in spring as yellow and red
spheres - the females at the growing tips, the males, further
back. The red female flowers ripen to become large hanging
balls of seed remaining on the tree throughout the winter. The
London plane grows to 100ft (30m) and, when allowed, will
have a broad spreading crown with thick, twisting boughs. The
characteristic bark is smooth and peeling to reveal lighter
creamy patches underneath.

Plane tree encourages fine judgement - the ability to discern
the truth of a situation. This justice, wisdom and calm clarity
derives from a deep tuning into the nature of things. Plane

helps to develop a mental structure that is able to cope with the flow of intuition and information.

The essence has a beneficial effect on the Small Intestine meridian preventing too much introspection or dwelling on sadness. It can be useful for those who are prone to over-analyse and who are subject to fits of melancholy.

The Gall Bladder meridian is also strengthened and this can create a state of detachment where a broader viewpoint can be seen. Again a peacefulness replaces anxiety and intellectual or organisational over-analysis.

The mental body is relaxed and becomes more open to deeper perceptions and meditative states. Plane tree creates a calm, detached space in which to grow.

Signature: Retaining its seed capsules: memory, information, facts. The ability to respond positively to outside influences (withstanding pollution, heavy pruning etc.), implies detachment and the ability to let go and see the larger perspective.

Comment: Plane trees, especially the oriental plane, have a long history of being venerated for their great size and age. It is said that the Persian emperor Darius halted on one of his campaigns to honour a plane tree with sumptuous offerings. This is hard to imagine if you know only the street trees - but find a free-spreading, unpruned mature tree and it is easy to get a better impression of the energy. Oriental planes, because they are so large and more sensitive to cool weather are less planted than the vigorous, tough hybrid. The London plane is another tree born in this country combining the energies of the Americas and Asia into a new form.

Plum
(Prunus domestica)

Key: EMPOWERMENT; DEEP PINK; HEALING LOVE; FREEDOM FROM BOUNDARIES; SELF-CONFIDENCE AND POWER; DYNAMIC, PRACTICAL CHANGE.

The plum is a common garden and orchard tree. Originally all plums were cultivated in the Middle East by crossing parents of different species. The plum, like its small-fruited varieties the damson and greengage, developed from crosses between the blackthorn and cherry plum. Plum flowers in April and May producing a white, five-petalled blossom that sprinkles the black branches just as the leaves are opening.

For such a small, domestic tree the plum spirit carries great healing power. The energy of plum is the transformation and transmutation of physical activity and material existence by healing, transcendent love. It can access the knowledge and understanding of creation through healing love and the desire to go beyond established boundaries.

There is a sense of freedom and space to achieve the perfect flow of information, communication and peace. It gives the space and freedom to establish peace. Fears are easier dealt with through understanding their causes and through a clearer use of the intellect - the creative aspect of the rational mind.

The Triple Warmer and Central meridians are supported, helping to counter the ennervating emotions of shame and loneliness. There is a clearer understanding of one's place in the universe and an increased awareness of the relationship to all created things, as well as a better ability to express what the heart feels and to experience bliss.

Plum

The throat chakra is energised strengthening the sense of personal power, allowing one to accept things as they are and help to bring about practical solutions. The base chakra is also allowed to play a greater part in practical, everyday decision-making, particularly giving access to the instincts. Although a great deal of spiritual energy is brought in with the plum essence it is directed towards dynamic and practical ends.

Signature: Bred for sweetness, kept close as sustenance.

Pittespora

Píttespoꞧa
(Pittesporum tenuifolium)

Key: IN TWO MINDS; CLARITY OF PERCEPTION; CLARITY OF MIND; SENSE OF HUMOUR.

This tree is native to the forests between the mountains and the sea of New Zealand's coastline. It can be found in Britain where the winters are mild. Pittespora can grow to 33ft (10m) in a neat, compact, broadly columnar form. The leaves are evergreen with glossy surfaces and a characteristic pronounced wavy margin. It flowers in late spring with small waxy, fragrant deep red-purple petals and bright yellow anthers. Except on the variegated varieties, these flowers can be inconspicuous from a distance.

Pittespora brings clarity of perception and clarity of mind. It gives the ability to see the truth from a broader viewpoint and to act on it in an orderly, organised way.

When one is "in two minds" and unable to determine where loyalties lie, this essence helps to clarify how we really feel. This releases pressure from the Kidney meridian and also balances the spiritual body.

The clarity and creativity at the finer levels of the self helps to relax anxieties, over-seriousness and lack of humour.

With the new, clearer perspective it is easier to explore what one is really about at a core level. This increases the sense of purpose, mental peace and encourages a truly individual way to be alive.

Signature: The red/purple and yellow flowers suggest the balance of energy between the head(purple) and gut (yellow) levels of reaction. The flowers sit close to the leaf axils, between leaf and stem, and therefore are between two different forms of expression. Just as the tree itself grows in the area between mountains and sea. Hesitancy is suggested by the strongly wavy leaf edges.

Comment: Pittespora is quite a common garden and park tree in the South West of England as the climate tends towards milder winters. It can also be found in Ireland and southern England.

Privet
(Ligustrum vulgare, Ligustrum ovalifolium)

Key: OLD WOUNDS; HEALING SUBTLE BODIES; RELEASE OF DEEP SHOCK; ORANGE.

Privet is best known as a hedging plant and this species is *Ligustrum ovalifolium* introduced from Japan in the 1840's to largely replace the native species, *Ligustrum vulgare*. Both plants are similar in form and habit except the native species has smaller leaves and flowers and does not retain its leaves in winter like the Japanese variety.

Wild privet can be found in hedgerows and woods. Both types bear a dense head of white flowers in July. The scent is strong and carries far in warm weather, though not to everyone's favour as it has a sharp echo to its heavy sweetness. The flowers form shiny black berries in autumn, once used in dyeing. Privet can reach a height of about 10ft.(3m), tends to be shrubby with straight stems of hard, off-white wood.

Privet works primarily at the level of the subtle bodies though there is a slight energising of the meridian system. The main areas it affects are the emotional, astral and causal bodies - that is, the levels of feeling and emotion; the personality and ego; and the collective awareness and past-life influences.

There is an increase in energy and life-force in the emotional body that helps the acceptance of growth and change. The astral body is helped to recognise the need to release blocks caused by the physical trauma in this or other lifetimes.

Privet is not particularly effective at emotional levels. It has more focus on physical, structural patterns of programming,

235

Privet

and is indicated whenever there is a need to release shock from within the subtle bodies. A harmonious vibration is created and this helps to heal and balance the subtle anatomy.

The emotional body very often deals with the individual's reaction to both itself and others. When this is brought into a finer balance with the astral body and the causal body, it becomes clearer which behaviour patterns are simply echoes from distant encounters - a reliving of past dramas. Once this is realised it becomes easier to disengage the automatic responses and see the situation from the present viewpoint. Such rebalancing will also help to put the individual at ease where they may feel out of place.

Signature: The privet can be trimmed, shaped and cut throughout the year without harm. It reminds us that wounds and restrictions need not damage us permanently and that recovery is always possible.

Red Chestnut

Red Chestnut
(Aesculus x carnea)

Key: FEAR FOR OTHERS; SECURITY; DETACHMENT
FROM OUTCOMES; HAPPINESS IN THE PRESENT;
POSITIVITY; PHOBIAS; WORRY; RED-VIOLET.

The red chestnut is a hybrid between the horse chestnut and
the red buckeye from North America. It is thought to have
originated in Germany and was available in the 1820's.
Although a hybrid, it is fertile and breeds true, although most
trees are grafted onto the more robust horse chestnut. It is a
lighter, much smaller tree reaching a height of 22m (65ft) and
is not as long-lived. The leaves are smaller, darker and less
splayed than horse chestnut. The spikes of flowers are pink or
dark red and appear in May and June.

With red chestnut comes a feeling of security and protection at
a very deep level of being. There is a peace and detachment
from emotional issues to do with expectancy and hope. This
encourages the ability to live in the present rather than with
the possibilities of futures.

All the subtle bodies are brought into balance where fears and
needs are countered by the awareness of joy and happiness.
This arises because a sense of underlying security allows one to
deal with and balance up fears and anxieties.

Communication with others is made stronger, and without the
stabilising balance this essence brings, such close links might
upset personal equilibrium and boundaries.

There is a greater balance between the mind and the imagination. This again, helps to resolve fears and phobias caused by
experiences in the past.

There is an ability to manifest, or increase the possibility of manifestation, of what one thinks. It is therefore useful that red chestnut encourages a balanced positive view and breaks the hold of self-fulfilling worry.

Signature: The red candles suggest stability and strength of action carrying strong emotions effortlessly with the ability to discard or transform them where appropriate.

Reờ Oak
(Quercus rubra)

Key: PRACTICAL SUPPORT; STAMINA; INSTINCT; ATTACHMENT TO LIFE; RED-VIOLET.

The red oak is one of the largest deciduous trees in eastern North America. Mature trees grow to 90ft. (27m) with a girth of six to nine feet. The seedlings are the fastest growing of all the oaks - between 7-10ft.(3m) in five years. The leaves are characteristically oak-shaped but with sharp-pointed tips turning a red-orange brown in autumn. The catkins appear with the bright yellow new leaves and when fertilised the fruit forms acorns that take two years to ripen. The first recorded tree in England is in 1739, though here it rarely lives above 200 years.

The quality of red oak is energising and practical for the mind. It encourages exploration of practical or physical techniques with which to expand self-awareness, such as hatha yoga, Ch'i Kung, and so on.

Red oak energy is healing and strengthening to the skeletal system. It can increase the amount of energy and stamina available and aids in the assimilation of minerals needed to support the skeletal system. The healing functions of the bones, such as red blood cell production, is also enhanced.

The base chakra becomes more closely aligned to the energies of nature. There can be a deeper attachment to the Earth and a deep knowing about one's place and function. This is the nature of the instinctive, right-acting body personality that gives the "feeling" of what is right to be and do.

Red Oak

The solar plexus chakra is cleared of self-doubt and false self-concepts and is helped to speed the healing of all self-issues.

At the finest level red oak emphasises the awareness of the individual as a being that is loving and constantly loved. It can find practical outlets for the yearning towards Unity. It will help with the lesson of learning to let go of what is dearest, so that one can be given everything in return.

Signature: The strong earthy-red colouration of the autumn leaves that remain on the tree for many winter months.

Rowan

Rowan
(Sorbus aucuparia)

Key: NATURE; CLEARING OF PERCEPTION; CO-CREATING; MERGING; MEMORY; SPACE TO THINK AND LISTEN; COSMIC LINKS; GREEN-VIOLET.

The rowan, also known as the mountain ash, grows at a higher altitude than any other native British tree. In the north its autumn foliage is the brightest of reds, though further south they fall early. Rowan is familiar from the masses of red berries the tree bears from midsummer onwards. The leaves consist of pairs of stalkless leaflets with forward-pointing serrations. In May rowan has clusters of creamy white flowers with a warm, musky-sweet smell. It is usually a delicate, airy tree that can grow to 65ft (20m.).

Rowan enhances the ability to tune into the energies of nature. This is because it encourages focus and discipline and a clearing of perception that allows breakthroughs in awareness in order to contact deeper levels of universal consciousness. This broader perception is balanced with the ability to ground information and communication in an integrated and supportive manner.

Rowan helps to overcome illusions and encourage realistic spiritual aims and great creativity. The essence will even foster greater co-creativity as the limited self becomes submerged in its greater nature.

The Large Intestine meridian is stimulated helping to calm the emotions and overcome feelings of separation. Letting go and forgiving allows hidden qualities to be contacted. Fears can be uncovered and dissolved.

The heart chakra is filled with a nurturing serenity whilst the crown chakra is enabled to solve emotional blocks and re-configure awareness in a larger, more spacious and supportive environment. The higher chakra, the tenth, is brought to a state of purity, openness, expansion and emptiness, where the universal can easily flow into the individual.

The fine subtle bodies, the causal and the spiritual, are ener-gised though the effects tend to be practical: there can be an improvement in memory and a quietening down of over-excited thought processes. Memory recall is stimulated as is the ability to communicate with deep intuitive levels.

The spiritual body is cleansed of trauma and this can have a healing effect at the physical level on allergies and physical shock as it brings harmony to the immune system. At the same time such cleansing allows a better contact with devas and Earth spirits.

There is an increase in satisfaction and happiness. More space to think and identify needs.

The quality of opening up awareness to the universe means that rowan creates a connection to the "fixed stars", very distant objects, which brings a deeper understanding of the cosmos and the ability to recognise and make use of that energy in a positive, creative way.

Signature: Growing in lonely, high, mountainous regions rowan mediates between the ethereal and the physical, like a yogi in solitary retreat.

Scots Pine
(Pinus sylvestris)

Key: PENETRATING INSIGHT; BREATHING EASY; CLEANSING; HEART AND BROW CHAKRAS; UNDER-STANDING; SUBTLE SIGHT; TENACITY; PATIENCE; INDIGO-GREEN.

The Scots pine is a pioneer tree that survives well on poor or sandy soil because it has many mycorrhizal fungi that provide nutrients and minerals, particularly phosphorus. These fungi may also help the tree against pathogens, in exchange getting organic compounds and sugars from the tree. There are many different forms of Scots pine but those most planted are the tall, straight forms. Although native in the Scottish Highlands, Scots pine was only re-introduced into England around 1660 when trees were planted in North Hampshire. From there it quickly spread over the heathlands of Berkshire and Surrey. Until replaced by American softwoods Scots pine was the main forestry tree, its wood, oil and extracts providing many different products.

Scots pine flowers in May and June producing huge amounts of pollen (second only to elm). The red-pink female flowers appear at the tip of the most vigorous growing shoots. These, when fertilised, will ripen over the next three seasons, releasing the wing-like seeds as the cones are alternately wetted and dried. The male flowers are bright yellow and cluster around slower growing shoots.

The pyramidal young trees lose their lower branches as they mature eventually taking on the familiar flat and spreading crown on a long bare trunk. They can grow to 120ft (36m) and live for not much more than 150 years.

Scots Pine

The activity of Scots pine focuses on the upper parts of the body. At a physical level the essence can help create calm and relaxation in the chest areas, both relaxing and clearing the lungs, easing breathing and reducing stress from the heart.

It is a cleansing, clearing energy that can help release blockages anywhere in the system. Boundaries are both repaired and maintained, so that individual integrity is enhanced without blocking out energy or information from other sources.

As the boundaries become more secure the heart is opened and calmed and the brow chakra can become greatly energised. This enables a clearer perception of fine levels of energy such as auric and clairvoyant sight. The perception of nature and the kingdoms of nature, especially nature spirits, are made more accessible. But clarity of the brow chakra also functions at the mundane, or anyway less spectacular, levels of seeing. Thus there is a clarity of understanding - "seeing" at every level, and this means that meditative states are easier to maintain and tend to be more profound. Scots pine brings a penetrating insight and allows a balanced growth of individual gifts. It increases tenacity and patience with the ability to see the broader aspects of good and bad. With this, too, comes forgiveness. Scots pine effectively grounds excess energy and ensures a practical development of this mental clarity, avoiding a top-heavy build-up in the body.

Signature: Though rooted in the soil the usual focus of many pine trees is at the top of the tree, as the essence focuses at the top of the head.

Comment: Many of the Caledonian pines have significantly longer limbs branching at lower levels, greatly changing the familiar visual appearance.They have a greater weight, gravity and sense of presence. Unfortunately, few areas now have these original stands and natural regeneration is largely prevented by the widespread grazing of deer herds.

Edward Bach used a boiled preparation of the male and female flowers to clear guilt, the sense of blame and the failure to live up to one's expectations. It clears emotional confusion caused by an unclear understanding of the situation.

All pines give a resin by tapping the trees. It is used for making turpentine and rosin. The impure resin is tar produced especially from the roots, it has been used as an antiseptic and stimulant. The essential oil is produced by distillation of the wood by steam under pressure. Pine is a rubefacient, diuretic and irritant. It has been used for bladder, kidney and rheumatic problems and for clearing the mucous membranes of the respiratory system. Recently, a bark extract, pycnogenol, has been found to be the most effective remover of antioxidants and free radicals from the body.

Silver Birch
(Betula pendula, Betula pubescens)

Key: BEAUTY; CALM; GOODNESS OF BEING; TOLERANCE; HARMONIOUS SHARING; CREATIVE EXPRESSION.

The two native birches, the silver birch and the downy birch occupy different environmental niches and have distinct forms although cross-breeding occurs between them. Energetically they bring very similar energies as expressed through the focus of the land.

The droopy-branched silver birch has a tall, pointed crown with a delicate, weightless and supple appearance. Mature trees are characterised by the silver-white bark marked with black. The leaves have flat bases and alternate larger and smaller teeth. Silver birch favours dry, sandy soils. It can reach 100ft (15m) but is more often half this size. Birches are short lived, usually no longer than 100 years, and have the characteristic hardiness and rapid growth of pioneer species.

Downy birch favours heavier, wetter soils so where silver birch occupies valley sides and heathland, downy birch can more often be found in valley bottoms, marshy ground and closer to water. The tree is sturdier, less tall (up to 80ft, 24m), and has fewer, thicker and less pendulous branches. The bark tends to be darker but can also be silver, and the leaves have more even teeth and a triangular base. As its name suggests the stalks are hairy whereas the silver birch is hairless.

The spirit of birch brings the ability to experience beauty and calmness. The name of the tree derives from the Indo-European root "bharg" which means bright, shining, white. The experience of beauty is more than a simple appreciation of form: it is

Silver Birch

an acknowledgement and realisation that everything that is, rejoices in its own nature, its own life - that simply being is sufficient to create endless joy within oneself. Beauty is the acknowledgement of this simple goodness of being, both in oneself and in others. Without the awareness of beauty there can be only separation and division.

Encouraging this quality birch helps to ease harsh judgements of the self and of others. It can give the ability to understand and accept other people's views without criticism. Supporting individuality and nurturing life feeds one's surroundings and reflects back life-supporting energy into oneself.

Harmonious sharing is encouraged. This state then allows the further growth and manifestation of new beginnings and new possibilities for great happiness. Birch will be of use to those who find it difficult to express themselves.

The experience of quiet and deep beauty helps to release old patterns of behaviour. Beauty is the experience of the transcendent within the present, and as such this essence effectively dissolves the rigidity and stubbornness that prevents clarity and flexibility of action and perception.

Signature: Birch is a pioneer tree that provides a fertile environment for many other forms of life - to which it will eventually give way. The quality of flexibility and grace is apparent in the form. Another form of flexibility appears in the slight modification of characteristics between the two species in their different habitats.

Comment: Birch has always been connected to concepts of brightness - in terms of fire (birch wood burns very brightly), and in terms of colouration, habitat and spiritual energy. Birchwoods are very light places and many other species can grow up underneath protected by the birch trees and fed by their rotted leaf litter. The white bark stands out clearly like a torch or way marker. The slender grace of birches seems feminine to many and they have been long connected with both nurturing Mother goddesses (many of whose names also spring from the same roots and signify fire, brightness, whiteness such as Brigid, Bride, Beorc, Birkana), and with goddesses of death - white also having obvious correlations with dead flesh, bone, winter and cold.

Understanding the harmony between these concepts is the key to experiencing beauty as a permanent reality of perception, rather than as a fleeting glimpse of something beyond greatness. The birch spirit confronts each person with unglamourised reality, with things just as they are: with death as well as life. It can begin to move us towards a position where beauty spontaneously shines through everything, instead of our continual defining of things as good or bad. Birch is a tree of tantric teachings. It allows us to work with everything in front of us in our lives, both what we love and fear, in order to taste the real taste of experience which is essentially as sweet as the sap of the birch, and as sustaining.

The relationship of birch with the fly agaric mushroom (*Amanita muscaria*), which is its favoured host, is also one that repays deeper investigation. This fungus has an undisputed history of magical and shamanic use. It, too, has a form that allows associations of both male and female gender, a reputation of death, danger and exaltation and a connection to light. This unpredictable mushroom spirit can bring to its human communicant discomfort and oblivion (though not death of the body) or an increasing bliss that climaxes in the experience of a celestial light flooding down onto the head. This light, together with the red and white-flecked cap, blood and bone, life and death, menstrual blood and semen, its appearance after fertilising rains in autumn, all reinforce and strengthen the constellation of associations that birch itself conjures up.

Silver Maple
(Acer saccerinum)

Key: MOODS; BALANCED MERIDIANS; REDUCES TURBULENCE; BLOOD CHEMISTRY; SWEETNESS; STABILITY; BLUE-PINK.

Many maples can be found planted throughout Britain for their decorative colours and shapes. Silver maple comes from the eastern coast of North America where it is one of the main sources of sugar and maple syrup, extracted from the sap in springtime. In Britain the sugar content is not high enough for this use, but silver maple is one of the most widely planted as it is hardy (especially in the south of Britain), and grows to 100ft (30m) with an open crown that casts little shade. Silver maple flowers in early spring with small reddish flowers appearing on the shoots before the leaves open. Silver maple can be easily identified by its rounded, deeply lobed leaves and irregular teeth. The undersides show silver-green in the wind giving the tree a subtle, shifting colouration.

Silver maple essence helps to balance the flow of energy through the body. It is particularly useful for integrating the various meridians into a more balanced flow. Silver maple reduces energy blocks and turbulence, increasing the vitality and life-energy available at any one time.

Mood swings can be regulated and evened out, particularly where they are initiated by chemical factors within the blood chemistry. A change of mood affects the constituents of the blood and similarly an excess of some chemicals can alter mood. Silver maple helps to speed up the normalisation of blood chemistry and also seems to strengthen many aspects of the circulatory system.

Silver Maple

Where there is a harshness experienced in one's moods, or where there is sensitivity to food substances that results in mood swings, such as hyperactivity or lethargy, this essence can help the body to restore balance.

Like all maples, silver maple has an energy that increases the experience of stability and sweetness in life.

Signature: The sweet, sugar-rich sap of silver maple: the flow of life-energy and sustenance through the body's subtle channels and circulatory systems. Changing moods: the shifting colours as the leaves are turned in the breeze to reveal the light undersides and then the darker tops of the leaves.

Spindle

Spindle
(Euonymus europaeus)

Key: SELF-INTEGRATION; KNOWING SELF; PERSONAL DIRECTION; THE SHADOW; TRANSFORMATION; TRANSMUTATION OF NEGATIVE STATES; WHITE-GOLD.

A small tree growing to 20ft, spindle has a neat, fine form, which although quite common in hedgerows, makes it pretty inconspicuous. Young stems are identifiable by having alternate vertical stripes of green and grey-brown bark. In summer there are a profusion of four-petalled, star-like flowers of greenish white that become unmistakable four-lobed red fruits containing orange seeds in autumn. Given the right autumn weather spindle leaves can turn to a dark red. The yellow, smooth, tight-grained wood was formerly used for spindles, pegs and cages. All parts are highly emetic and purgative.

There is peace and balance: a communication with deep levels of intuitive mind regarding one's place and direction. Individual nature attunes to the Higher Self allowing self-expression in accord with one's true nature without negative, egotistical feelings of superiority. This helps to remove the tendency to judge others, to be competitive, the need to succeed or be first at every opportunity - a stabilising of Lung meridian functions.

Heart and solar plexus chakras work together enabling a discernment of a true purpose, a way of life, in which one feels at home and motivated to achieve. The brow chakra is energised for finer levels of perception and communication.

The astral body, the integrated personality vehicle, is helped to cleanse the energy patterns of negativity and separation from the personality. A great energising on soul levels.

259

There is an ability to look at and understand the deepest, darkest, most hidden parts of the self. To understand and accept the Shadow self. The Shadow is that which we have decided is not us, the traits and qualities that have been rejected through every stage of our lives, which are as defining and as much a part of our constructed self-image as those qualities we readily identify with.

To bring light and wisdom into the most hidden levels of existence. Transformation and awareness of what appears negative. Apparent negativity is able to be absorbed and transmuted. Those energies within the self that have been suppressed through fear are relaxed so that stagnant, negative energy can be transformed into life-supporting, dynamic energy.

Signature: The red fruits open to reveal the orange seeds within (colour of healing wisdom); a revealing of the core/ seed/ potential by means of understanding and action (red-pink fruit). A plant unknown to many, which once recognised, can be seen everywhere. Keeping itself to itself, spindle tree has none-theless a strong spirit and unique energy.

Comment: The wahoo, or Indian arrow-wood, common in the eastern United States, is a variety of spindle most used in medicine. In small doses the bark is used to stimulate appetite and digestion. In larger doses, like the European species, it is highly irritating to the gut and is a strong purgative. This is used where there has been some liver disorders where it stimulates production of bile and is a tonic. The Latin name, deriving from the name of the mother of the Furies, Euonyme, gives a good indication of the force of this tree's effect on the body!

260

Stag's Horn Sumach
(Rhus typhina)

Key: MEDITATION; HEAD CHAKRAS; FLOW OF INTUITION; COOLING MIND AND EMOTIONS; FLOW OF INFORMATION; VIOLET.

Stag's horn sumach is native to meadows, scrub and woodland margins of eastern North America. It may have got its name from the Sumac Indians who were familiar with the tree and its many properties. The stems were used as tobacco pipes and tubes, the fruits eaten and the bark used as a healing astringent and antiseptic. It was brought to Britain in 1629 by John Parkinson, an apothecary who used a root extract to treat fevers.

It is a small tree growing to 26ft (8m) with an open crown and widely spreading habit. It throws up suckers all around the base, though because it can be cut back heavily, it is a common garden tree. The leaves are long with many toothed leaflets. Stag's horn sumach flowers in summer usually with male and female spikes on separate trees, the male a loose cluster of greenish-yellow flowers, the female a tighter spike of rusty red. These ripen into fruit with a sour but edible taste and remain on the furry stems all winter.

The essence of stag's horn sumach has an effect of releasing tension in the neck and throat areas. At subtle levels too, this tree focuses on the head centres. The brow chakra and related minor chakras are energised, as is the mental body. This has a general positive effect on the functioning of the endocrine system via the controlling pituitary gland.

It enables the flow of intuition and expression of the Higher Will. This is because it activates the mental body where belief

261

Stag's Horn Sumach

systems, reality models and self-images are held. Sumach initiates a calmness and non-attachment on emotional levels that allows more freedom to access valid supportive actions (hence useful for determining "spiritual direction"), particularly when in a meditative state.

Stag's horn sumach is an excellent tree to help balance the energies for meditation. It is cooling, stilling the mental and emotional processes and allowing an easier flow of information and energy together with an increased awareness of underlying reality and the ability to perceive harmonious and unifying characteristics of existence.

Signature: The purple-red branches and flower spikes: the chakras of the head.
Its use as a tube and pipe stem: a conduit for life-energy (smoke/breath) and sweetness (maple syrup was tapped from the trunk via a sumach stem).

Comment: Except poison ivy, all members of the Rhus family have been known for their healing properties for many centuries. They are very high in tannins so are effective astringents useful in cases of diarrhoea, fever, skin complaints, dysentery. The berries are also a coolant and diuretic.

Strawberry Tree

Strawberry Tree
(Arbutus unedo)

Key: QUIETUDE; CROWN CHAKRA; IMAGINATION; REDUCING THOUGHT PROCESSES; FLUIDITY; WHITE.

This is a small tree growing to 30ft (9m) with a short trunk often lying along the ground and with twisting branches. Its distribution is patchy but is truly native in south-west Ireland where it grows on seaward cliffs. Elsewhere in Britain it grows well in sheltered places, though is usually shrubby. The evergreen leaves are regular, toothed with a white central vein. Strawberry tree flowers in September and October with green-white heather-like flowers hanging in loose clusters. The fruit takes two years to ripen, beginning as small green globes, then expanding to yellow and finally red, fleshy spheres. Ripe fruit and flowers can be seen together. The fruit is quite edible though too subtle for some tastes.

Strawberry tree has a focused and specific effect. It primarily stimulates the crown chakra increasing potential for healing and personal spiritual growth. The qualities of the imagination and inspiration are encouraged.

The mind is quietened and cleared. Strawberry tree can almost instantly reduce the levels of mental noise to the merest whisper. It is experienced as a sudden whitening or clearing of thought from the head. This is not calming as such - the emotions are not involved, simply a reduction in noticeable thought processes is allowed.

Transformation occurs through this stillness and silence. As movement and activity dictates all form, it requires a cessation of activity and movement in order to effect change. Ceasing to move allows form to become more fluid and less bound. This can create an opportunity to clear the effects of past actions, habits, and routine thought patterns.

Signature: Appearing so late in the year the soft white flowers and different stages of ripened fruit are like a snapshot in time-the year suspended, as thoughts are also suspended.

Comment: Seeing a mature strawberry tree in full autumn sunshine with bright red fruits, yellow orange fruit, milky bunches of flowers amid glossy deep green leaves brings to mind those Otherworldly Celtic trees who bear fruit and flowers simultaneously, or who bear all kinds (colours) of fruit, or that are alternately burning with flame and bursting into greenery. Altogether a magical tree that is just about hanging on to very small pockets of habitat throughout Europe as though it is a remnant of much older times.

Strawberry tree is generally unhappy in northerly and easterly winds and thrives best in shelter. In and around Devon it is a common sight, though one of the largest trees to be seen is opposite Sueno's Stone in Forres, in the far north of Scotland on the Moray Firth.

Sweet Chestnut
(Castanea sativa)

Key: THE NOW; DEEP PEACE; RELEASE OF SHOCK; WELL-BEING; PHYSICALITY; ACCEPTING CHANGE; PINK.

Sweet chestnut, or Spanish chestnut, grows wild in southern Europe, North Africa and the Near East. It is particularly common in Spain. It was possibly brought to Britain by the Romans - its fruits are the edible chestnuts traditionally roasted in winter. Sweet chestnut is one of the largest broad-leaved trees in the land, though it does not germinate easily in the cooler British climate. It is a very fast-growing tree and can live for a long time. The tree grows tall and narrow with low branches that spread the crown wider with age. It can grow to 100ft. The larger trees develop a noticeable spiral twist in the bark. Male catkins appear in long yellow tassels in summer at the tips of the branches and the smaller green, rounded female flowers can be found near the leaf bases. The leaves are long, narrow and glossy green with saw-toothed edges. The fruits develop into paired nuts within a green prickly shell.

With sweet chestnut spirit there comes an intuitive under-standing of underlying harmony and balance. It becomes easier to communicate hidden emotions and feelings in a clear way. This allows deep peace into the heart and emotions. This essence also creates a detached space that enables one to regain the understanding that comes from a wider perspective.

Central and Heart meridians are balanced and this re-establishes centreing, focus and respect for the self. There is a release of stress, shock and trauma that allows creativity to flourish in a way that expresses the individual energy pattern. This can profoundly affect healing and growth on spiritual levels.

267

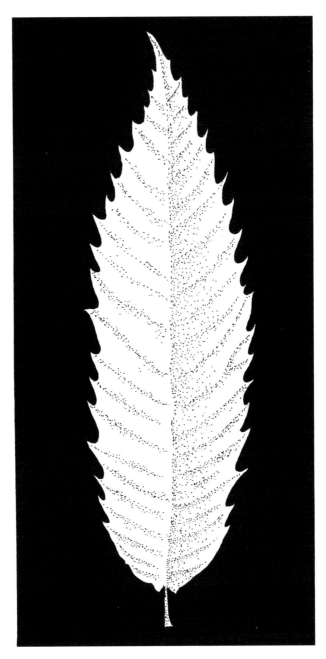

Sweet Chestnut

The brow chakra becomes better able to function, which makes it easier to formulate strategies and find creative ways out of difficult situations.

All the subtle bodies become more integrated and there is an increased confidence in the physical body, improving the sense of well-being. Validation of physical existence in this way helps to remove any sense of guilt and clarifies the personal awareness of right and wrong.

Sweet chestnut helps to release this deep guilt particularly where it focuses on a lack of love for physical existence, physicality itself, strong passions and desires and anything "earthy". It can be especially useful for those who feel uncomfortable about physicality as being "unspiritual". It encourages the truth that the physical is holy and not a "mistake". The essence also helps to bring the ability to accept change on the physical plane and creates a doorway whereby cosmic and universal loving energies can enter the physical system.

At the very finest level sweet chestnut brings love to all actions. There is an increase in confidence, peace and inner tranquillity. A space is created in the present for healing and love and protection against aggression.

Signature: The uncomfortable prickly case contains the sweet fruit: the joy and bliss within the apparent discomfort of physical form.

Comment: Sweet chestnut is among the oldest and largest living creatures in this land. A tree at Tortworth church in Gloucestershire is possibly the oldest with claims that it was planted in the reign of King Egbert who died in 839. It was certainly recorded as a very large tree in the 12th century and now has two massive branches lying along the ground that have sent up smaller trees or branches that appear to be layers from the original bole.

Edward Bach suggested that sweet chestnut be used for those who suffer unendurable anguish and face destruction and annihilation.

Sweet chestnut wood, when young, provides excellent timber with very little sapwood. It can be used to take the place of oak, and will last better than oak where it is under the ground. The leaves are picked in summer and dried or used fresh for convulsive coughs, such as whooping cough, and in other conditions where the lung tissues are irritated. It is astringent and tonic.

Sycamore
(Acer pseudoplatanus)

Key: LIGHTENING UP; SWEETNESS AND STRENGTH; ENERGY LEVELS; GENEROSITY; LETTING GO; EMOTIONAL STABILITY; ENJOYMENT OF LIFE; COMMUNICATION OF HEALING ENERGY; YELLOW.

The sycamore, great maple or great plane, is the largest of the maple family. It is native to the mountain chains of Europe where it grows in rich, damp soil singly or in groups. The date of its introduction to Britain is not known though sycamore is first mentioned in 1551. Sycamore is a fast growing tree that spreads rapidly tending to shade out other plants. It is a huge, spreading deciduous tree with a dense, domed crown of large, five lobed leaves that are dark green with a paler underside. It is hardy to pollution and salt-laden air and can live for around 500 years. The wood is white-yellow and easy to work but strong and hard. The flowers appear in long grape-like racemes of bright green just after the leaves in April, later forming the characteristic winged seeds. This large tree rarely grows over 100ft (30m), but develops huge trunks with pinkish brown bark that peels in irregular strips. Because of their size, fast growth and hardiness sycamores are important shelterbelt trees particularly in northern Britain.

The essence of sycamore deals with the powerful combination of sweetness and strength. On a physical level it can help with the assimilation of nutrients through the actions of the pancreas and small intestine. There can also be some beneficial strengthening of the legs. As with other maples there is a better regulation of energy levels to make the most of available resources, so sycamore can be of use where there is chronic tiredness or lethargy.

Sycamore

There is an increase in the awareness of the sweetness of life, which encourages further growth and fulfilment. All the meridians are strengthened, but particularly the Bladder meridian, encouraging the positive emotional states of peace, harmony, balance and the resolution of conflicts. The Circulation-Sex meridian also brings the ability to relax, to become more generous and giving and to be able to let go of past issues and events rather than hanging onto them and basing the present moment on past attitudes and outcomes.

The throat, brow and crown chakras are activated. These centres will bring a broader view, clearer insight and a greater ability to make changes that matter. There is thus an overall increase in empowering information and understanding.

A minor chakra located near the pancreas is also affected that not only helps to balance the physical functions of that organ but also creates a greater emotional stability by inducing calm.

All the subtle bodies are brought into a better alignment with each other, but sycamore particularly focuses on the mental and spiritual bodies. In this way the physical and emotional results (the relaxation and greater enjoyment of life), can be understood to arise from a shift of understanding, a more positive appreciation of experience that derives from the mental bodies. These bodies hold the belief structures and ideas of what is our personal status and reality.

Greater acceptance, tolerance and understanding emerges in emotional and mental states. Once this release and relaxation begins it is easier to experience the main energy of the sycamore spirit, which is the activation of the potential to communicate healing energy and to know that one is sustained and protected by the deepest universal levels of love and understanding.

Comment: Many people consider sycamore to be little more than a weed, crowding out other, more appropriate "native" trees. It is true that sycamore has few niches for other species, yet its fast growth and excellent wood, not to mention the wonderful biomass, would make it a fine forest timber tree for hardwood. Its no good just moaning about its tenacious success: looking at sycamore from a positive angle it could at least provide many resources efficiently and quickly. And it's a great climbing tree!

TamaRisk
(Tamarix gallica/anglica)

Key: FIRE OF TRANSFORMATION; TOTAL FREEDOM; TOTAL FLEXIBILITY; SOLAR PLEXUS; DEEP CLEANSING; HEALING OF TRAUMA; WHITE.

Familiar on southern coastlines, especially when it bears spikes of pink flowers in summer, tamarisk originates from the Middle East where it was recognised for its medicinal properties. Tamarisk was introduced to Britain as a healing herb in 1582 and has become naturalised in coastal areas where its tolerance to salt and dry climates helps it thrive in harsh conditions. The delicate feathery foliage and mass of flowers have made varieties of tamarisk popular as garden plants. Flowering tamarisk resembles nothing so much as wafts of pink, wind-blown sea foam borne on green feathery waves.

Tamarisk essence is about understanding one's place at the centre of creation. It brings the awareness of one's emergence from the Absolute, and place within the Absolute, even when in the midst of the relative worlds. Because of this knowledge there is total freedom, total flexibility, complete understanding that all is possible. The divine spark leaping from the central sun of Being.

It tunes the energies of the solar plexus chakra into intelligent and evolutionary ways to direct the personal will, life-force, personality and lifestyle. It can be like harnessing for the Higher Self one's own chariot of power.

The spiritual body is cleansed and healed, which increases clarity in personal energy on the finest of levels. This will tend to cleanse and transform the ability to manifest and use the finest spiritual energies (the "ethers"), so that these can be

Tamarisk

integrated into the net of the energy field. Thus there is the possibility of deep cleansing and the healing of profound shock.

An essence for spiritual direction, freeing up energies for personal expansion and growth. Tamarisk is uplifting and helps shift age-old dross so that the true self can emerge. To paraphrase the Upanishads: "burning the seeds of karma in the furnace of Being".

Signature: Growing by the ocean tamarisk is between two worlds, land and sea. The ocean of possibilities is within its experience and it is adapted to the force that the ocean can display.

Tree Lichen

Tree Lichen
(Usnea subfloridana)

Key: WISDOM; PURIFYING; WATCHFUL; KNOWLEDGE OF
THE PAST; FREEDOM FROM TIME AND SPACE;
INDEPENDENCE; LUNGS; VIOLET-WHITE.

Lichens of various shapes and sizes grow on trees where
pollution levels are low and other environmental conditions are
suitable. The temperate rainforests of north-west America, for
example, and the high altitude woods of Dartmoor are home to
an abundance of lichen species. Though not a tree itself, the
lichen that lives on the branches of trees partake of the
ambient energy of their surroundings. Slow growing, living for
many years and dwelling in that borderland of definition,
neither in contact with the earth yet relying on the rootedness
of trees, they consist of two symbiotic plants with distinct
healing qualities. Usnea is strongly antifungal and anti-
microbial - properties which are thought to protect and
strengthen the trees upon which they grow. The usnea species
are all many branched, long and often beard-like grey-green
plants.

The energy of tree lichen is particularly powerful and its
wisdom is profound. The primary energy is purifying and
protecting, and indeed it has been said that usnea's prime
purpose is to support and protect the life of the trees.
It brings the ability to let go of anything no longer needed in
order to grow more fully. There comes a greater knowledge and
understanding, (particularly on a "feeling" level), of the cyclical
nature of time and events.

An integration of the mental, causal and spiritual bodies brings
knowledge of the soul outside time. There is an improved
ability to access past knowledge and ancient wisdom. Indeed

this freedom from the construct of time and space allows one to communicate with beings beyond the solar system. It brings the ability of going everywhere without going anywhere.

All the chakras can be brought into balance including the minor chakras in the centre of the palms that stimulate the heart and kidneys, and small chakras in the centre of the ears that help to open and cleanse physical pathways such as the nose, sinuses, lungs and so on. A general process of purification and cleansing is encouraged.

Tree lichen is an ethereal essence that is rooted in physical existence and the knowledge of the past. It brings a sense of independence and detachment without isolation.

Signature: Growing in shade, particularly on the north side of trees, tree lichen has affinity to the Pole Star which itself is the doorway to understanding and experiencing the whole universe. Tree lichen has access to Earth energy indirectly through the tree but lives fully open to cosmic energies. The branching quality of the usnea species resembles both the structure of the nerve pathways in the brain and the fine passageways of the lungs.

Comment: Tree lichen is an immensely profound doorway to many tree kingdoms and other ecological realities. At a physical level its effectiveness at combating serious bacterial infection, such as tuberculosis, has been shown to be remarkable. Many fungal and bacterial infections respond well to the herb. Yet lichen of all sorts needs a clean environment and temperate climates to thrive and it can easily be damaged. If you wish to work with lichen spirit be aware that it takes centuries to grow large and that it is a vital aspect of the Earth's immune system. Collect only small fragments that have already fallen or been blown from the tree.

Tree of Heaven
(Ailanthus altissima)

Key: HEAVEN ON EARTH; PRACTICAL SPIRITUALITY; SPIRITUAL BLOCKS; CROWN CHAKRA; DRAWING SPIRIT INTO PHYSICAL; HEALING OLD EMOTIONS; RED-VIOLET.

The tree of heaven originates from China and was introduced into Britain in 1751. It does well in mild climates and is planted as an ornamental tree in many towns. In very warm climates it seeds and suckers freely. Tree of heaven resembles ash, with opposite leaflets, but distinguished by a notch on each near the stalk, and often there is no terminal leaflet. The leaves open red very late, usually at the end of June, and also fall early. Trees are separately male and female with flowers of greenish-yellow clusters forming large pannicles at the end of the shoots. The female flowers ripen to a red-brown winged fruit. Tree of heaven is an open crowned, broadly columnar tree with "wriggly" branches growing to 65ft (20m).

Tree of heaven gives dynamic, energising spiritual qualities whilst protecting the integrity of the subtle body systems. It brings practical spirituality and practical wisdom.

The crown chakra becomes energised and grounded so that its energy is more easily accessible to other systems of the body. It supplies sufficient energy that this essence will help to break through any blocks at the spiritual level.

Minor chakras at the centre of the forehead help to clarify the understanding of larger truths and ideals, universal concepts and past life viewing. A chakra at the medulla oblongata is stimulated to integrate the experience of bliss onto the physical, thus allowing the experience of the spiritual into the physical.

Tree of Heaven

There is the ability to resolve emotional trauma and obsolete emotional beliefs held in the emotional body. Within the finer levels of personal consciousness there is a greater possibility for the integration and healing of subtle injuries and shock.

Comment: The inner bark of the tree of heaven was used in China for dysentery and other bowel complaints. It has a strong, bitter smell and is astringent, antispasmodic and a cardiac depressant. A tincture from the root bark has been used for asthma, epilepsy and cardiac palpitations.

Tulip Tree

Tulip Tree
(Liridendron tulipifera)

Key: SPIRITUAL NOURISHMENT; SELF-EXPRESSION; SOLAR PLEXUS; GNAWING EMPTINESS; SORROW; THROAT CHAKRA; CREATIVITY; COMMUNICATION; BLUE-YELLOW.

The tulip tree, tulip poplar or yellow poplar is native to the eastern United States. It is fast-growing and can reach a height of 50ft in ten or eleven years. It will flower after twenty years and continues to flower for a further two hundred years. It is a tall tree that can grow up to 120ft (37m). It was first planted in Britain in the second half of the 17th century in Fulham. The tree is named for its tulip-like flowers that open greenish-yellow with a blush of orange and pink in mild climates. The leaves are a unique four-lobed shape on long stalks that allow them to flutter like poplar leaves in any breeze.

Tulip tree essence encourages practical outlets for thought processes and wisdom from the Higher Self. There is increased motivation for self-expression.
At a physical level the essence brings cleansing and calming to the abdominal organs, and the pancreas in particular. There is a relaxation of tensions in this area.

It balances the Stomach meridian, which brings nourishment at spiritual levels. Where there is spiritual hunger, a gnawing emptiness, tulip tree will bring the means to fulfil personal creativity whilst also bringing increased feelings of connectedness and belonging.

The Small Intestine meridian is also affected. There is relief from sorrow and an increase in peace and understanding. This can also strengthen the links to the spirit worlds.

It is possible to remove deep blocks to personal creativity and expression with this essence. Tulip tree will strongly affect the balance of the throat chakra. Artistic abilities will be more likely to manifest and there will generally be an increase in mental creativity and communication skills. The release of long-term stresses encourages greater depths of meditative experiences and an increased clarity and peace. Strong emotional responses, particularly spontaneous reactions, are able to be easier controlled and less volatile in nature.

Signature: This is a tall, narrow tree that flowers from the lowest branches to the top of the crown. Although not conspicuous in colouring the flowers are large and elegant in shape and suggest the flowering of skills at many different levels of awareness.

Comment: The bark of the tulip tree produces a quinine-like, bitter compound.

Víbuꞧnum
(Viburnum tinus)

Key: REASSURANCE; EMOTIONAL PEACE; BALANCED ASSERTIVENESS; INNER CONFLICTS; SERIOUS ILLNESS; POSITIVITY; PINK.

Viburnum tinus is native to southern Europe and the Mediterranean. It is a large evergreen shrub or small tree with waxy, white clusters of sweet smelling flowers that appear as long lived clusters in autumn and over winter into springtime, depending on the weather conditions.

The main code of this essence is emotional peace, the flow of peace and an easy communication of feelings. Viburnum helps to find practical ways to establish one's place and feel supported. There is the growth of a balanced assertiveness and an integration and expression of one's own sense of peace and how the world is perceived. This results from a strengthening of the Governing meridian, which dictates the quality of support an individual feels, and the Gall Bladder meridian in its aspect of encouraging humility.

Mental activity and individual belief systems are integrated in order to deepen levels of perception and real peace. Inner conflicts will tend to be understood and eased.

At a much finer level, where we initiate the tendencies to act in certain ways, there is a healing of deep trauma. The energy of viburnum is able to initiate extremely deep levels of healing and will help to re-integrate fragmentation caused by near-death experiences and life threatening situations. Working with the causal and mental bodies viburnum eases any sense of vulnerability, sensitivity, neuroses, feelings of being unhappy or unsettled.

287

Viburnum

Reassurance and the re-evaluation of past experiences in the light of a broader, more positive outlook is encouraged.

From the underlying connecting energy of all consciousness, there comes a communication from the heart of things.

Signature: The subtle, sweet smelling flowers during winter.

Comment: Viburnum tinus is one of the many viburnums to find a place in parks and gardens. Tinus is the most common of the winter flowering varieties. Like many ornamental species, its particular energy signature is so ubiquitous that it plays a significant stabilising role in the urban environments into which it has been introduced.

Wayfaring Tree

Wayfaring Tree
(Viburnum lantana)

Key: FAR MEMORY; PSYCHOMETRY; HEART; PROTECTIVE SPACE; SUPPORTIVE; ANCESTORS; TYING THINGS TOGETHER; GREEN-VIOLET.

Named thus by Gerard in the sixteenth century because of its prevalence along the lanes of southern England, its older name is "hoarwithy" ("white plant stem"). A small shrub tree, it is easily identified from its strong-looking opposite leaves on short, stout stems. In May and June a dense umbel of white flowers appears on each branch-ending, ripening to shiny black berries. Hoarwithy prefers dry alkaline soils and is rarely found in the North of Britain.

This essence links to specific memories of the place where it is growing. It recognises and calls up similarities of circumstance and patterns that are repeating in the present. Indirectly this can give access to the mechanisms for remembering personal past existences. Wayfaring tree may also help with other temporal sensitivity as in psychic archaeology and psychometry. Working with the tree in situ can be very revealing of times past.

The heart energies are cleared and lightened of emotional burdens such as fear, jealousy, envy etc. There is an ability to focus on choices for life direction and growth.

The etheric body is strengthened, re-establishing its boundaries and independence. This creates a protective space that encourages health of the physical body.

An increased balance of internal energies and polarities that supports information to flow in from other dimensions.

Protection against negatively and pollution. Integration with planetary awarenesses. The essence is supportive of changes in spiritual life.

Signature: found on old paths and uplands-where our ancestors established themselves first. Strong, heart-shaped leaves. Extreme flexibility of stems-even greater than hazel. "Tying things together".

Comment: We were hunting for wayfaring tree for ages before we found it. In our part of Devon it can't be found, though twenty or thirty miles away it is pretty common. Finally we made an essence from trees growing high on the Hampshire Downs. We love this plant-simple, strong and unobtrusive. A few days after making the essence we were walking in an Exeter park very familiar to us and there it was in a hidden border - a large wayfaring tree in full flower!

Weeping Willow
(Salix babylonica)

Key: EGO; BALANCING EXTREMES; CYNICISM; CONTEMPT; SELF-RIGHTEOUSNESS; INCREASED GENEROSITY AND UNDERSTANDING; BELIEF-SYSTEMS; EQUAL TO ALL, SUPERIOR TO NOTHING.

A tree everybody recognises, weeping willow originates from China where it grows near rivers and watercourses with other willows and poplars. It was thought to have moved westwards along the Silk Route as woven baskets and crates. Willow twigs, even those apparently dead, will grow quickly when stuck in the ground. It was probably introduced into Britain at the beginning of the eighteenth century from a tree growing on the river Euphrates. All willows cross-fertilise and present day weeping willows are much larger than their Chinese forebears.

Like most willows, weeping willow has a deep link to the solar energies. Its main focus is the balancing of power. Power can be both life-supporting and life-damaging, like gentle sunlight or the fierce desert sun. Weeping willow helps to balance the extremes of energy. At its finest level it is the spiritual fire, the manifestation of wisdom and beneficial energy to all.

It works with aspects of the Spleen and Lung meridian energy. The essence deals with the negative ego-based states of cynicism and contempt - both of which originate from a false sense of self-righteousness, or at best a failure to accept other people's views as valid.

The emotions and passions are helped to quieten, increasing generosity to others and calms agitated or bad-tempered states.

Weeping Willow

Weeping willow will help to ameliorate the contempt that arises because one fears that one is perhaps wrong, or that a personal world-view is not unassailable and may, indeed, be invalid. It brings on new creative freedom and the strength to accept another point of view.

The etheric body is given support, particularly to those areas where there is some belief system difficulty with that body part or system. Thus the essence can help to mend the underlying breaches in all-accepting love and compassion that can allow serious disease to manifest.

Useful in situations of emotional hurt and sense of loss, it helps re-establish one's true worth and value within creation: equal to all, but superior to nothing.

Signature: Open branches that reach sunwards and are happy to cascade down to earth. The cascades of leaves forms a safe curtained space - a flexible border or barrier to the outside world. A fountain of force expressing the strength and flexibility of water.

Whitebeam

Whitebeam
(Sorbus aria)

Key: OTHERWORLDS; FINE LEVELS OF PERCEPTION; AWARENESS; ALERT; CONTACT WITH THE WORLDS OF NATURE; SHIFTING LEVELS; REVEALING THE HIDDEN; INDIGO.

Whitebeam is native to limestone and chalk landscapes though because of its modest, neat size, resistance to pollution and attractive appearance, it is widely planted in town streets and parks. Whitebeam can grow to 80ft (24m) in these situations, though it is usually smaller in the wild. It is an easily identified tree with large oval leaves that have green-grey hairy undersides. In early spring the light green buds appear like candle flames. When the new leaves are fully unfurled the umbels of creamy upright flowers open in May. These will ripen into bright scarlet berries that are rapidly eaten by birds.

Whitebeam stimulates fine levels of perception. It will energise the sacral, heart and brow chakras and a minor chakra just above the medulla oblongata, helping to balance creativity and insight with a keen awareness and alertness.

The mental and astral bodies are aligned to work with fine perceptions, so that one can begin to learn how to shift energy levels. Whitebeam brings a deeper attachment and understanding of the animal and plant kingdoms. It can also encourage contact and understanding of the natural world from the desire to be of service and to heal.

The essence increases one's harmony with cosmic energies and it opens the heart to recognise the underlying energy that supports all life. Whitebeam in this way strengthens the personal field whilst at the same time opening it up to experience, or float between other dimensions or angles of reality. A fine tuning of the energy fields occurs so as to be able to see and hear what is usually hidden.

Signature: The ephemeral shimmering of whitebeam's large soft leaves on a sunny spring day, particularly where the large creamy flowers are showing, makes the tree appear otherworldly, as if it is not quite all within this physical reality.

White Poplar
(Populus alba)

Key: STARTING AGAIN; SURE FOUNDATIONS; CONFIDENCE; HEART CHAKRA; RELATIONSHIPS; POSITIVE CHANGE; EMOTIONAL STATES; PINK.

White poplar originates from the southern parts of Europe and western Asia. The date of its introduction to Britain is unknown but white poplar has certainly been planted as an ornamental tree since the 16th century. It rarely grows above 65ft (20m) and tends to have a leaning trunk and an asymmetrical crown. Like all poplars the leaves tremble in the breeze, and the almost white undersides create a silvery shimmering. The bark too, is easily identified: the upper trunk is silver with dark lozenge or nail-head markings. Both male and female flowers are woolly catkins. The male are crimson and the female are green and appear on separate trees before the leaves appear.

White poplar essence brings the security from which to grow outwards, express oneself and find new ways of being and thinking. Once there is established this sure foundation in confidence and self-worth it becomes easier to explore many different possiblities.

White poplar energises and heals the heart chakra so that there is an increased determination to recover from setbacks - particularly where they are of an emotional nature. Relationships, both with others and with oneself, are given a boost of energy through practical growth and expansiveness.

There is wisdom, intelligent energy, creativity and healing focused on how one sees the world and one's place in the world. White poplar can bring the ability to make positive changes

White Poplar

that are new directions, perhaps unthought of before, more in line with one's true desires and strengths.

Overall the essence brings an increase of wisdom, joy and contentment.

Signature: The alternation of dark green upper leaves and silver-white lower surfaces; the dark lower bark and the patterned upper trunk, both suggest a transformation of emotional states.

White Willow

White Willow
(Salix alba)

Key: TRUE SELF; WHOLE BEING; SOLAR PLEXUS; CLEAR UNDERSTANDING; BROADER PERSPECTIVES; RELATIONSHIP OF SELF TO CREATION; CLEANSING; CLARIFYING; VIOLET.

White willow is the largest of the British willows growing to 80ft (25m) and forming an open, but often narrow crown of large boughs. The long thin leaves have silvery hairs that are particularly dense on the undersides giving the tree its characteristic colour. Like all willows, it is fast-growing but fairly short lived, only rarely surviving to 100 years unless pollarded. The male and female flowers appear on separate trees in spring as the young leaves emerge. Male catkins are yellow and females green, later producing fluffy white seeds that are distributed on the wind.

White willow is characterised by the understanding and development of awareness of the whole being. It is able to access deep levels of knowledge, communication and devotion at many dimensional levels.

The solar plexus chakra is brought more energy that allows it to cleanse itself. This is at a level of a subtle cleansing, balancing the complementary energies of spirit and matter, energising the finest areas of potential and nudging them towards physical manifestation. In this particular combination, spirit is more enabled to infuse the individual being so that the influence of the smaller self, or ego, is taken out of the equation. When the personal influence lessens it is easier to become a clear channel for more universal energies.

At the same time the brow chakra is supported and its qualities enhanced. There is a greater clarification of all levels of communication and understanding, and the mental processes are allowed to perceive finer levels of reality.

Smaller chakras at the medulla oblongata and centre of the forehead are also activated resulting in the ability to see oneself within a broader perspective, as part of a larger pattern. This allows the self to be brought to a truer balance within itself. It also helps to prevent incorrect assumptions or arrogance about one's state of knowledge. White willow will balance those aspects of life that are either too narrowly fixed on a mundane level or too rarified at a spiritual level. It will bring a more balanced vision of life in all its aspects.

Overall, there is a clarification and clearing of one's relationship to the universe, to the whole. With this can be experienced a sense of bliss or bliss consciousness, with love welling up to flavour all perceptions with its integrating energy.

Signature: The silver-white foliage catches the eye like a tall, growing fountain. The cleansing and clarifying nature of this essence is represented by this silver shimmering. The open, many boughed form of the larger willows echoes the relaxation and openness to universal energies that the spirit of willow brings down to an individual, personal level.

Wych Elm
(Ulmus glabra)

Key: ATTAINMENT; ANALYSIS; STUDY; ORGANISATION; UPLIFTING MOODS; CONFIDENCE IN ABILITIES; EXPRESSION; PEACEFUL AWARENESS; MEDITATION; YELLOW-VIOLET.

The wych elm, also known as the mountain elm, is native to the British Isles and grows further north than any other elm. It thrives on deep, damp soils. It is less susceptible to Dutch elm disease but it too can suffer. The leaves are hairy and very rough to the touch, have a clearly pointed tip and a very unequal base. Unlike other elms the wych elm when young has a smooth, pale grey bark when the other elms have light brown, heavily fissured and "scabby" looking bark. Wych elm, given the space, is a much wider tree than other elms but grows less tall with a maximum of about 100ft (30m). The flowers open on the shoots in February and March developing into apple-green bunches of seedcases, clearly visible before the leaves emerge. Wych elm is resistant to city pollution and so was widely planted in the towns of Scotland.

The essence of wych elm helps to bring the mind to clarity, allowing analysis and understanding of subtle thought processes. This makes it a useful energy to employ in any study situation. Organisation and expression of material becomes easier as the logical and intuitive parts of the mind work side by side.

There is a positive, more life-affirming outlook and a lifting of mood that would be helpful where there is pessimism or depression.

Wych Elm

The Gall Bladder meridian is strengthened in such a way that there can be a clear assessment of one's worth and place in the world. Wych elm brings a confidence in personal abilities and strengths.

Of the subtle bodies, the emotional body is most affected. There is a greater calm and balance within which it becomes very much easier to get thoughts and feelings across to others.

At a spiritual level wych elm increases the ability to communicate and understand many different aspects of universal energy. There is a growth in peaceful awareness, no matter what state one is experiencing at the time. Wych elm can be used for meditation as it not only creates stable awareness but allows the consciousness to touch many subtle realms.

Yellow Buckeye

Yellow Buckeye
(Aesculus flava)

Key: DEVAS; INNER AND OUTER WORLDS; CROWN CHAKRA; NEW IDEAS; NATURE SPIRITS; INDIGO.

Yellow buckeye, also called sweet buckeye, is superficially similar to horse chestnut though smaller in size. The crown narrows and the smooth trunk carries twisting, drooping branches with palmate leaves. In spring the yellow flowers are produced in candle-like clusters. The buckeyes are native to the river valleys of the eastern United States - along the Ohio and among the Alleghany and Appalachian Mountains. It was introduced into Britain in the mid 18th century.

There is an integration and harmony between the environment and one's interior energy systems. At the level of feeling there is a correspondence and interchange between oneself and one's surroundings. This forms easier links to devic energies and the ability to understand and integrate that level of consciousness. The tree itself tends to act as a focus for anchoring devas to a location so it naturally augments contact with devic and elemental levels.

The crown chakra is enabled to understand different levels of communication and thought. There is the ability to frame new images and concepts in a logical, understandable way. The spiritual body is similarly tuned.

At the level of emotion, there is an activation of enthusiasm, drive and comprehending one's true needs.

Yew

Yew
(Taxus baccata,
Taxus baccata "fastigiata")

Key: PROTECTION; SURVIVAL; ENERGY INTEGRITY; GROUNDING; BASE CHAKRA; ENERGY; MOTIVATION; INTEGRATION WITH PLANET; BROW CHAKRA; VISIONARY; RED.

The yew is among the most ancient of trees and is certainly the longest lived tree in Europe, if not the world. It is resistant to most pests and conditions except flood, and because of the inherent strength and flexibility of the wood, will carry large boughs without breaking. Yew is not a tall tree growing to about 50ft (15m), but where allowed it will spread widely resting its lower boughs on the ground and even re-rooting itself to send up daughter trees. The dark green, shiny flat needles are familiar in most churchyards, as are the red arils - the fruit of the female trees in autumn. Female flowers are small and inconspicuous whilst male flowers can be seen in early spring, bright yellow and yielding huge amounts of pollen. A natural variety found by a farmer in County Fermanagh in the 1770's is the origin of the Irish yew, a stately towering upright yew with many straight "spires". All Irish yews derive from this single find in the wild.

Yew essence is the paramount energy to use with all issues of survival and protection. It activates and strengthens all organs and systems that have to do with maintaining energy levels and energy integrity, so it naturally tends to enhance the circulatory system and the immune system, particularly the liver functions. It can also give more energy to help the absorption of nutrients.

Depending on the status of the individual system yew essence can either increase or regulate available energy levels. As it is profoundly grounding, those who are unused to being grounded may take some time to adjust to the differences of feeling and perception.

The base chakra is enlivened with all the resultant qualities that brings: increased motivation, drive, energy, practicality, strength and focus on the present, as well as protection from external energy intrusions. The solar plexus chakra also is enhanced, and together these chakras protect from harm by activating the highest spiritual values of survival and protection. This includes the activation of far memory, discrimination skills and deeper understanding of one's relationship to the planet and to the sun and its energy influence. Once securely rooted into the planetary field it becomes possible with yew essence to explore many different times and places, accessing patterns held within the land and within the yew tree itself. This often directs the energy to the brow chakra where visionary experiences are processed and perceived.

Signature: The longevity and ability of yew trees to put on new growth, even after apparent death. The flexibility and strength of the wood and its red colouration.

Comment: An extract from yew bark, called taxol, has been found to prevent the growth of cancer cells. This finding threatened the existence of the remaining mature yews growing in the North West Coast forests of North America, which were cut and stripped of bark. Luckily it has now been found possible to extract the chemical from branch clippings. Hopefully this will prevent the extinction of perhaps the oldest living beings on this planet, the yew trees. The ages of churchyard yews are probably greatly underestimated. Growth is slow and erratic and not easy to measure. In many instances, however, it is more than likely that the church was sited near sacred yews rather than vice versa.

Index

We are keen to avoid a 'recipe book' approach to healing with trees, we think it is greatly preferable to encourage readers to form their own correspandences and associations. However, to start you off the following index lists the keywords we have covered in the book with page references. You are strongly encouraged to experiment and make notes on what works for you.

Abdomen, 29, 121, 129, 136, 149
Ability To Reach Goals, 131
Accept And Let Go, 219
Accepting Change, 267
Aching Heart, 123
Activation of Self-healing
    Processes, 223
Agitation, 155, 157
Alert, 297
Alienation, 223
Analysis, 32, 305
Ancestors, 291-292
Anxiety, 30, 69, 71, 83, 107, 154,
    161, 175, 204, 213, 228
Apollo, 81-82
Appropriate Change, 173
Artistic Activity, 169, 171
Artistic Creativity, 205, 207
Assuredness, 42, 153
Attachment To Life, 241
Attainment, 305
Awareness, 1, 6-8, 13, 16, 18, 33,
    38, 50-51, 60, 62-63, 75, 124,
    137, 139, 142, 153, 159, 169, 179-
    181, 183, 185, 189, 199, 203, 210,
    213, 229, 235, 239, 243, 245-246,
    253, 260, 263, 269, 273, 275, 286,
    297, 303, 305, 307

Balance After Shock, 123
Balance & Discrimination, 99-100

Balance of Mind, 103, 147
Balance of Purpose, 73
Balanced Assertiveness, 287
Balanced Meridians, 255
Balanced Relationships, 219
Balancing and Regulating Heart
    Chakra, 141
Base Chakra, 29, 77, 93, 173,
    216, 231, 241, 311-312
Beauty; Calm, 251
Belief-systems, 17, 293
Belonging To Earth, 223
Block Release, 81
Blood Chemistry, 255
Blue - Indigo, 163
Blue, 33, 36, 155, 163, 207
Blue-gold, 143, 227
Blue-orange, 103, 169
Blue-pink, 255
Blue-yellow, 147, 285
Body Relaxes, 87
Boundless, 51, 193
Brainfood, 143, 145
Breathing Easy, 247
Brightness, 193, 253-254
Bring Forth and Balance, 215
Broad Understanding, 219
Broader Perspectives, 303
Brow Chakra, 32-33, 105, 121,
    148, 174, 205, 207, 249, 259,
    261, 269, 304, 311-312

Calm, 55, 89, 117-118, 121, 125,
127, 137, 139, 151, 155, 157,
161, 187, 189, 199, 203, 205,
221, 227-228, 245, 249, 251,
273, 307
Calming and Supporting, 181
Calms Fears, 221
Change, 10, 13, 21-23, 26-27, 29,
31, 45, 49, 51-53, 59, 62-63,
101, 118, 127, 136, 173-174,
181, 183, 185, 203, 225, 229,
235, 255, 265, 267, 269, 299
Channelling, 105, 163, 165
Circulation of Energy, 93
Clarifying, 303-304
Clarity, 13, 65, 71, 73, 75, 95, 105,
111-112, 127, 131, 133, 155, 157,
173-174, 186-187, 198, 205, 211,
221, 227, 233, 249, 253, 275, 286,
305
Cleansing, 47, 71, 75, 82, 95, 101,
127, 131, 197, 246-247, 249, 275,
277, 280, 285, 303-304
Clear Decision Making, 129
Clear Understanding, 77, 303
Clearing of Perception, 245
Clears Nervous System, 221
Co-creating, 245
Comfort; Nourishing, 191
Communication, 11, 13, 31, 105,
107, 113, 118, 129, 143, 145, 148,
153, 163, 169, 174, 217, 221, 229,
239, 245, 259, 271, 285-287, 289,
303-304, 309
Communication of Healing Energy,
271
Compassion, 54, 121, 125, 175, 185,
203, 209, 213, 295
Competance, 149
Complete Security, 89
Composure, 175
Confidence, 30, 40, 43, 52, 62, 83,
85, 91, 97, 107, 154, 175, 193,
195, 205, 207, 221, 225, 269, 299,
305, 307
Confidence In Abilities, 305

Confusion and Fatigue Eases, 119
Confusion, 38, 54, 101, 119, 121,
131, 185, 250
Connectedness, 97, 100, 105, 205,
207, 285
Constructive Energy of Anger, 209
Contact With The Worlds of Nature,
297
Contempt, 43, 293, 295
Contentment, 43, 113, 124, 148,
301
Continuity of Awareness, 203
Cooling Mind and Emotions, 261
Core Behaviour Patterns, 153
Core Strengths, 193
Cosmic Links, 245
Courage, 41, 159
Creative Energy, 185, 211
Creative Expression, 210, 251
Creative Intelligence, 185-186, 193
Creativity, 29, 83, 85, 118, 125,
129-130, 136, 148-149, 169, 171,
185-186, 192-193, 205, 207, 219,
233, 245, 267, 285-286, 297, 299
Crown Chakra, 7, 33, 105, 107,
123, 157, 185, 187, 211, 246, 265,
281, 309
Curiosity, 21, 199
Cycles of Time, 203
Cynicism, 293
Cynics and Critics, 209

Decision-making, 153-154, 231
Deep Cleansing, 275, 277
Deep Peace, 109, 133, 148, 199,
207, 221, 267
Deep Pink, 229
Deep Red-magenta, 209
Deep Red, 81, 89, 199
Deeply Energising, 223, 225
Depression, 43, 111, 305
Despair, 43, 85, 101, 136
Detachment From Outcomes, 239
Detachment From Past, 111

Detachment From The Source of
Pain, 209
Determination, 173-174, 299
Detoxification, 73, 167
Devas, 246, 309
Development, 1, 27, 103, 165, 181,
249, 303
Discernment, 89, 163, 259
Drained and Over-emotional
States, 119
Drawing Spirit Into Physical, 281
Dynamic Mind, 137
Dynamic, 24, 27, 31, 36, 57, 71,
121, 137, 153-154, 186, 216, 229,
231, 260, 281

Easy-going, 83, 85
Ego; Balancing Extremes, 293
Emotional Healing, 87, 209
Emotional Peace, 199, 287
Emotional Stability, 223, 271, 273
Emotional States, 20, 41, 94, 273,
299, 301
Empowerment, 211, 213, 229
Energising Body, 137
Energy and Enthusiasm For Life,
199
Energy Boost, 81
Energy, 4-13, 17-33, 35-41, 44-46,
48-65, 67-68, 71, 73, 75, 81-82,
85, 91, 93-95, 97, 99, 103, 105,
109, 117, 119, 123-125, 129, 131,
133, 135-137, 142, 145, 149, 151,
153-155, 157, 159-160, 165, 169,
171, 173, 179-180, 183, 185-186,
191, 193, 197, 199, 201, 203-204,
207, 209-211, 213, 215-217, 219-
220, 225, 228-229, 231, 233, 235,
241, 246, 249, 253, 255, 257, 259-
260, 263, 267, 271, 273, 275, 277,
279-281, 287, 289, 293, 297-299,
303-305, 307, 309, 311-312
Energy Integrity, 95, 311
Energy Levels, 33, 44, 59, 94, 97,
216, 271, 297, 311-312
Enjoyment of Life, 271, 273

Enlivening, 1, 111, 181, 211, 213
Enthusiasm, 62, 119, 193, 199, 221,
309
Equal To All, 293, 295
Expansion, 4, 31, 61, 124, 137, 175,
193, 199, 201, 216-217, 246, 277
Expansion of Conscious
Awareness, 137
Exploration, 61, 77, 169, 177, 199,
217, 241, 313
Expression, 11-12, 31-32, 41, 50-51,
82-83, 85, 88, 100, 149, 154, 163,
169, 187, 193, 197, 210, 223, 234,
251, 261, 286-287, 305
Extremes of Emotion, 181

Far Memory, 291, 312
Fear, 29, 41, 54, 56, 62, 66, 100,
127, 161, 199, 223, 239, 254, 260,
291
Fear For Others, 239
Feeling, 13, 20, 29, 67, 87, 97, 109,
121, 135, 159, 193, 211, 235, 239,
241, 279, 309, 312
Fierce Compassion, 203
Fiery, 81-82
Fine Judgement, 227
Fine Levels of Information, 119
Fine Levels of Perception, 297
Fine Perceptions, 89, 297
Fire of Transformation, 275
Flexibility, 4, 15, 35-36, 38, 77, 79,
113, 118, 129, 174, 179, 219, 253,
275, 292, 295, 311-312
Flexible Communication, 129
Flow of Information, 85, 155, 229,
261, 263
Flow of Intuition, 155, 228, 261
Flow of Positive Energy, 95

Flow, 13, 24, 29, 31, 40-41, 47, 52-
53, 56, 58, 60, 62, 69, 71, 75, 81,
85, 91, 95, 100, 109, 123, 125,
129, 151, 153, 155, 157, 192, 197,
207, 213, 217, 221, 228-229, 246,
255, 257, 261, 263, 287, 291

315

Flowering of Skills, 143, 286
Fluidity, 265
For Delicate Energies, 159
Force of New Life, 93
Forgiveness, 42, 44, 88, 91, 117, 129, 141, 175, 249
Free Flow of Energy, 125
Freedom, 175, 177, 187, 201, 209, 213, 229, 263, 275, 279-280, 295
Freedom From Boundaries, 229
Freedom From Time and Space, 279
Fretful Children, 117
Frustration, 4, 16, 42, 135-136, 149

Generosity, 43, 207, 271, 293
Gnawing Emptiness, 285
Goodness of Being, 251, 253
Green, 4, 6, 69, 72, 95, 101, 107, 111-112, 117, 119, 123, 125, 129, 143, 147, 149, 153, 167, 175, 177, 185, 187, 191, 203, 205, 207, 209, 211, 215, 219, 259, 265-267, 271, 275, 297, 299, 301, 303, 311, 313-314
Green-gold, 131
Green-orange, 129
Green-red, 199
Green-violet, 245, 291
Green-yellow, 137, 161, 181
Grounding, 33, 81, 203, 216, 223, 311-312
Growth of Awareness, 63, 181
Growth of Creative Potential, 167
Growth, 63, 73, 79, 89, 115, 119, 123-124, 127, 135, 139, 141, 149, 154, 157, 160, 167, 171, 173-175, 181, 183, 185, 189, 197, 199, 201, 204, 207, 211, 215-217, 235, 249, 251, 253, 265, 267, 271, 273-274, 277, 287, 291, 299, 307, 312-313
Guide and Protector, 161
Guilt, 42, 49, 53, 75, 87, 121, 159, 250, 269

Happiness In The Present, 239

Happiness, 28, 37, 42, 71, 73, 87, 99-100, 187, 189, 193, 211, 221, 225, 239, 246, 253
Happy With Oneself, 191
Harmonious Sharing, 251, 253
Harmony With Surroundings, 77
Head Chakras, 261
Head, 11, 24, 27, 33, 37, 41, 44, 55-56, 71, 79, 83, 89, 95, 103, 105, 137, 148, 175, 183, 216, 233, 235, 249, 254, 261, 263, 265
Healing Emotions, 159, 191
Healing Love, 211, 229
Healing of Trauma, 275
Healing Old Emotions, 281
Healing Subtle Bodies, 235
Heart and Brow Chakras, 118, 247, 297
Heart Centre, 141-142, 199
Heart Chakra, 23, 31, 71, 75, 77, 93, 123-124, 131, 141-142, 161, 187, 246, 299
Heart, 12, 23-24, 28, 31, 40, 43-44, 49, 51, 55-56, 71, 73, 75, 77, 81, 91, 93, 109, 118, 121, 123-124, 131, 133, 135, 139, 141-142, 154, 159, 161, 179, 183, 187, 189, 191, 199, 201, 213, 215, 229, 246-247, 249, 259, 267, 280, 289, 291, 297, 299
Heaven on Earth, 281
Hidden Fears, 161
Hope, 43, 83, 93, 135-136, 217, 239
Humour, 87, 111, 175, 193, 233

Ideas, 135-136, 143, 145, 163, 171, 185, 197, 207, 210, 219, 273, 309, 313
Identification, 25, 73, 89, 113, 121, 197-198
Imagination, 8, 15, 26, 103, 207, 213, 239, 265
In Two Minds, 233
Increased Generosity and Understanding, 293
Increased Life-energy, 69

316

Increased Peace, 99, 147
Independence, 111, 279-280, 291
Indigo-green, 247
Indigo, 89, 163, 297, 309
Information Flow, 197
Inner and Outer Worlds, 309
Inner Conflicts, 287
Innovation, 199
Insight, 15, 33, 103, 117, 247, 249, 273, 297
Inspiration, 75, 103, 107, 135-136, 143, 145, 165, 171, 185-186, 213, 265
Instinct, 241
Integrated Spirituality, 199
Integration of Energy Systems and Environment, 179
Integration of Heart and Mind, 135
Integration With Planet, 311
Internal Clarity, 173-174
Internal Structures of Creativity, 83
Internal Sweetness, 193, 195
Intuition and Advice, 131
Intuitive Knowledge, 227
Irritability, 147-148

Joy, 44, 71, 85, 93, 99, 111-112, 135-136, 154, 168-169, 181, 193, 213, 221, 223, 225, 239, 253, 269, 301

Keeping At Bay, 81
Kindness, 185
Knowing Self, 259
Knowledge of The Past, 279-280
Learning From Experience, 185
Let Things Be, 113
Letting Go, 43, 97, 101, 167-168, 245, 271
Lightening Up, 271
Lightness and Joy, 181
Love, 3, 31, 41-42, 44, 76, 79, 87, 91, 117, 121, 123-124, 129, 141-142, 159, 209, 211, 223, 229, 254, 269, 273, 292, 295, 304

Lungs, 31, 131, 249, 279-280
Lust For Life, 73, 75

Manifestation, 5, 11, 38, 51, 53, 93, 186, 215, 240, 253, 293, 303
Meditation, 6-7, 28, 63, 261, 263, 305, 307, 313-314
Meditative States, 18, 227-228, 249
Melancholics, 227
Memory, 0, 10, 32, 51, 203-204, 228, 245-246, 291, 312
Merging, 245
Moods, 37, 255, 257, 305
Motivation, 29, 54, 73, 193, 215-216, 221, 285, 311-312

Nature, 32, 50-52, 54, 57, 59, 62, 75, 83, 85, 115, 133, 142, 163, 179, 186, 191, 198, 227, 241, 245, 249, 253, 259, 279, 286, 297, 299, 304, 309
Nature Spirits, 142, 179, 249, 309
Negative Emotions, 42-43, 149, 223
New Ideas, 136, 163, 309

Old Wounds, 235
Open and Relaxed, 187
Openness and Honesty, 191
Openness, 83, 163, 191, 246, 304
Opportunities, 153
Optimism, 93, 167
Orange, 69, 83, 93, 153, 235, 259-260, 266, 285
Orange-gold, 167, 171
Orange-red, 69

Orange, 69, 83, 93, 153, 235, 259-260, 266, 285
Orange-violet, 185
Organisation of Internal Harmony, 103
Organisation, 103, 198, 305
Original Thought, 163
Origins of Primal Energy, 215
Otherworlds, 76, 297
Out of The Woods, 131

317

Overseeing Love, 209
Overview, 119, 174, 199

Pain, 51, 62, 125, 209
Patience, 14, 217, 247, 249
Peace, 31, 42, 89, 99-101, 107, 109,
    111, 133, 147-149, 155, 157, 159,
    191, 197, 199, 207, 209, 221, 223,
    229, 233, 239, 259, 267, 269, 273,
    285-287
Peaceful Awareness, 305, 307
Penetrating Insight, 247, 249
Personal Direction, 259
Personal Energy Integrity, 95
Personal Path, 75, 131, 133
Personal Power, 139, 149, 220, 231
Phobias; Worry, 239
Physical Confidence, 205
Physicality, 125, 267, 269
Pink- Green, 141
Pink, 73, 112, 117, 123, 125, 141,
    159, 187, 191, 199, 229, 239, 267,
    275, 285, 287, 299
Pink-gold, 211
Pink-orange, 87
Pink-red, 203
Place of Calm Peace, 89
Pleasure In Physical Existence, 87-
    88
Poor Self-worth, 159
Positive Change, 21, 63, 299
Positivity, 97, 135, 167, 239, 287
Posture, 38, 179
Power of Peace, 147
Practical Change, 229
Practical Spirituality, 281
Practical Support, 241
Practicality, 119, 121, 216, 312
Protected Peace, 159
Protection From Negativity, 93
Protection, 5, 28, 64, 69, 71, 81-82,
    93, 159, 187, 203, 239, 269, 279,
    281, 292, 311-312
Protective Space, 291
Psychometry, 291
Purification and Integration, 191

Purification, 32, 95, 127, 191, 279,
    280

Quiet Enough To Hear, 101
Quiet Mind, 103
Quietude, 265

"Raison D'etre", 193
Re-integration After Deep Shock,
    147
Realistic Plans, 173
Reality Anchor, 215
Reassurance, 287, 289
Recognition of Required Action,
    173
Reconnecting With The Physical,
    125

Red-gold, 193
Red, 69, 72, 81-82, 89, 93, 112, 123,
    141, 143, 147-148, 153, 169, 199,
    201, 209, 215, 223, 227, 233, 238-
    243, 245, 254, 259-261, 265-266,
    281, 311-312
Red-violet, 239, 241, 281
Reduces Turbulence, 255
Reducing Thought Processes, 265
Reduction of Friction, 155
Relationship of Self To Creation,
    303
Relationships, 111, 124, 139, 169,
    191, 219, 299
Relaxation of Tension, 211

Relaxation, 38, 43, 71, 75, 83, 85,
    87, 101, 123, 129, 133, 167, 187,
    207, 211, 213, 221, 249, 273, 285,
    304
Release, 4, 69, 71, 81, 85, 89, 101,
    103, 109, 137, 149, 167-168, 191,
    197, 204, 207, 213, 235, 237, 249,
    253, 267, 269, 273, 286
Release of Deep Shock, 235
Release of Shock and Trauma, 167,
    267
Releasing Fears, 187

Removal of Deep Stresses, 205
Removal of Fears, 107
Resolution of Conflicts, 99, 273
Restlessness, 42, 135-136, 149, 187
Return To Centre, 123-124
Revealing Patterns of Behaviour,
  111
Revealing the Hidden, 297
Right Action, 50, 133, 153
Rooting Spirit Into Matter, 93

Sacral Chakra, 0, 29, 85, 151, 169,
  173, 185
Safe Within Self, 123
Secure Expansiveness, 193
Security, 43, 77, 79, 83, 89, 91, 100,
  107, 123, 135, 147-148, 151, 154,
  193, 195, 207, 216, 223, 239, 299
Self-awareness, 11, 88, 131, 133,
  153-154, 193, 241
Self-confidence and Power, 229
Self-expression, 191, 207, 259, 285
Self-integration, 259
Self-righteousness, 87, 293
Self-worth, 42, 73, 75, 117-118,
  154, 159, 191, 299
Sense of Humour, 87, 175, 233
Sensitivity, 13, 37, 85, 161, 197,
  257, 287, 291
Sensuality, 85, 87, 125
Serenity, 107, 109, 221, 246
Serious Illness, 287
Seven Chakras, 179
Shifting Levels, 297
Shyness Overcome, 107
Skills, 100, 127, 143, 183, 286, 312
Smoothness, 85, 197
Solar Logos, 113, 115
Solar Plexus Chakra, 30, 97, 123,
  125, 137, 154, 183, 219, 221, 243,
  275, 303, 312
Solar Plexus, 23-24, 30-31, 33, 71,
  83, 97, 118, 123, 125, 135-137,
  154, 157, 173, 183, 193, 207, 210,
  213, 219, 221, 243, 259, 275, 285,
  303, 312

Solid Growth, 135
Solidity, 29, 89, 151, 225
Solitude, 94, 175
Soothing, 125, 127, 163, 171
Sorrow, 37, 44, 95, 99, 285
Soul, 27, 39, 91, 97, 137, 159, 216,
  259, 279
Space To Think and Listen, 245
Spine, 27, 29, 41, 58, 179-180
Spiritual Blocks, 281
Spiritual Guide, 147
Spiritual Nourishment, 285
Spiritual Sun, 113
Spiritual Void, 219
Stabilising Emotions, 99
Stability, 27, 29, 37, 51, 69, 77,
  101, 117, 121, 136, 143, 149, 151,
  203, 216-217, 223, 240, 255, 257,
  271, 273
Stagnant Energy, 58, 131
Stamina, 241
Starting Again, 299
Steady, 79, 139, 155, 157, 187, 215
Stimulating, 21, 64, 81-82, 85, 113
Strength; Humour, 193
Strength, 62, 77, 93-94, 154, 193,
  240, 271, 295, 311-312
Stress Lifts From Heart, 141
Strong Emotions, 107, 183, 240
Study, 40, 143, 145, 305
Subtle Perception, 103
Subtle Sight, 247
Superior To Nothing, 293, 295
Supportive, 51, 54, 105, 133, 180,
  245-246, 263, 291-292
Sure Foundations, 299
Survival, 11, 29, 71, 93, 157, 311-
  312
Survivors of Natural Disasters, 223
Sweetness and Strength, 271
Sweetness, 29, 117, 127, 193, 195,
  231, 235, 255, 257, 263, 271, 273

Taking A Deep Breath, 101
Taking Back Control, 211
Talking To The Long Memory of

The Planet, 203-204
Tenacity, 247, 249
Tension, 29, 38, 43, 69, 71, 75, 83,
 85, 87, 130, 137, 148-149, 154,
 167, 204, 211, 213, 261
The Heart of Things, 73, 289
The Now, 267
The Path, 47, 173
The Shadow, 259-260
Throat Chakra, 31-32, 85, 107, 113,
 143, 154, 163, 167, 231, 285-286
Thwarted Personal Expression, 149
Times of Transition, 125
Tolerance and Love, 117
Tolerance, 38, 43, 87, 117, 129,
 175, 185, 219, 251, 273, 275
Too Hard On Self and Others, 129
Total Flexibility, 275
Total Freedom, 275
Transformation, 28, 118, 191, 229,
 259-260, 265, 275, 301
Transforms Aggression, 117
Transmutation of Negative States,
 259
True Feelings, 87, 107
True Self, 277, 303
Trust, 41, 58, 141, 175
Turmoil, 101, 131
Turquoise, 173
Tying Things Together, 291-292

Unblocking, 95
Understanding, 32, 41, 63, 67, 75,
 77, 87, 93, 97, 101, 105, 111, 117-
 119, 124, 127, 130, 133, 137, 139,
 155, 169, 187, 203, 207, 210, 213,
 219, 223, 229, 246-247, 249-250,
 254, 260, 267, 273, 275, 279-281,
 285, 293, 297, 303-305, 312
Understanding Needs of Self and
 Others, 137
Uplifting Moods, 305

View From The Still Centre, 89
Violet, 179-180, 261, 303
Violet-red, 205

Violet-white, 279
Visionary, 311-312
Vitality, 41, 77, 113, 115, 220, 255
Vulnerability, 187, 287

Watchful, 279
Weight of Responsibility, 129
Well-being, 37, 40, 49, 69, 71, 157,
 205, 267, 269
White-gold, 259
White, 73, 77, 87, 93-95, 107, 125,
 137, 141, 147-148, 155, 157, 173,
 179, 187, 193, 199, 209, 217, 221,
 229, 235, 245, 251, 253-254, 259,
 265-266, 275, 287, 291, 299-300,
 302-304
Whole Being, 303
Will To Express, 169, 197
Wisdom and Awareness, 169
Wisdom, 8, 54, 71, 75, 79, 89, 107,
 123, 127, 143, 157, 169, 171, 185,
 192, 219-220, 227, 260, 279, 281,
 285, 293, 299, 301
Wrath, 42, 209

Year of Moons, 77
Yellow-blue., 119
Yellow, 37, 72, 81, 89, 95, 97, 99,
 103, 113, 115, 123, 135, 137, 143,
 149, 161, 167-169, 175, 185, 197-
 198, 205, 207, 211, 215, 227, 233,
 241, 247, 259, 265-267, 271, 285,
 303, 308-309, 311
Yellow-green, 99, 149, 211
Yellow-violet, 305

Zest, 221

320

FOUR TREES: FOUR SPIRITS

" sound sequences for meditation and trance"

by Nemed

(James Binning, Simon Lilly,
Sue Lilly)

Four pieces of music designed to take you beyond normal consciousness and into attunement with specific spirits of the Tree Kingdoms.

Each side contains two 15 minute sound meditations that use particular note sequences and chants

Side A: 1. Yew   2. Elm
Side B: I. Oak   2. Holly with Ivy

Released through
ANEW MUSIC,
47 High Street, Harborne, Birmingham, B17 9NT
Tel: 0121 428 3138 email: drspear@fabs67.freeserve.co.uk

Tape or CD available from ANEW Music or
Green Man Tree Essences
c/o MCS, PO Box 6 Exminster, Exeter, Devon EX6 8YE
Tel: 01392 832005 email: info@greenmantrees.demon.co.uk

A selection of other Capall Bann titles. Free catalogue available.

Tree: Essence, Spirit and Teacher by Simon & Sue Lilly

Trees are the creators and maintainers of our reality. In every tradition their spiritual strength has been clearly recognised. Sue and Simon Lilly, developers of *"Green Man Tree Essences"*, share their experiences and describe a wide range of techniques by which we can come into a direct and powerful relationship with the Tree Kingdoms. Emphasis is placed on establishing a personal experience through which the teachings of the Tree Spirits can become apparent. Subjects covered include: The metaphysical reality of trees, Tree essences and how to use them; Meeting the Spirits - methods of communication; Tree Teacher Techniques; Attunements to forty different trees; Coming into the presence of tree energies through initiation, and an exploration of some powerful Tree Teachers. This is the first volume in the *"Tree Seer"* series. ISBN 186163 084 0   £15.95

Magical Guardians - Exploring the Spirit and Nature of Trees
by Philip Heselton

This is a book about trees, but a book with a difference, for it acknowledges trees to be wise beings who can teach us much if we approach them in the right way. This book shows how to go about it, revealing the origins of our awakening interest in - and love for - trees. Trees have a spiritual nature, and opening up to this spirit has been a constant feature in human society. Through practical guidance, this book gives hints on how we can make that contact for ourselves. The personalities of the ancient trees - our Magical Guardians - are explored, and the book reveals how we can start to acquire some of their deeper meanings. ISBN 1 86163 057 3   £11.95

The Enchanted Forest - The Magical Lore of Trees by Yvonne Aburrow

Fascinating & truly unique - a comprehensive guide to the magical, medicinal & craft uses, mythology, folklore, symbolism & weatherlore of trees. There are chapters on trees in myth & legend, tree spirits, trees in ritual magic, trees & alphabets (runes & Ogham) & weather lore. These chapters are followed by a comprehensive 'herbal index' with in-depth coverage of individual trees from acacia to aspen, wayfaring tree to willow. Profusely illustrated. *"..wonderful insight...easy to read...very informative, a lovely enchanting book". Touchstone magazine of OBOD* ISBN 1898307 083   £10.95

Healing Stones by Sue Phillips

There is an increasing interest in crystals, from collectors, magicians and healers, with correspondingly increased pressure on our earth's precious resources. Healing stones sets out a method that works on the same principles as crystal healing, but makes use of stones and pebbles that can be found lying around almost anywhere. Here is a chance to learn what any child knows instinctively - stones are magical. ISBN 186163 034 4   £8.95   **R98**

Crystal Doorways by Sue & Simon Lilly

Not yet another volume telling you everything you wanted to know about crystals. It focuses on a very particular system of using crystals and colour to bring about changes in your consciousness and an increasing understanding of the energy world around us. Developed as a result of running many courses, 'Crystal Doorways' gives a clear, immediately understandable, system of "energy nets" using small, easily obtainable crystals. These energy nets are simple, usually only requiring small tumbled stones, but they can be extremely powerful. Each net is illustrated and described in full, with what stones to use, where to place them, potential uses and background information. ISBN 1898307 98 9   £11.95

FREE DETAILED CATALOGUE

A detailed illustrated catalogue is available on request, SAE or International Postal Coupon appreciated. **Titles can be ordered direct from Capall Bann, post free in the UK** (cheque or PO with order) or from good bookshops and specialist outlets. Titles currently available include:

Auguries and Omens - The Magical Lore of Birds by Yvonne Aburrow
Caer Sidhe - Celtic Astrology and Astronomy by Michael Bayley
Celtic Lore & Druidic Ritual by Rhiannon Ryall
Earth Magic by Margaret McArthur
Enchanted Forest - The Magical Lore of Trees by Yvonne Aburrow
Familiars - Animal Powers of Britain by Anna Franklin
Healing Book (The) by Chris Thomas
Handbook For Pagan Healers by Liz Joan
Healing Homes by Jennifer Dent
Herbcraft - Shamanic & Ritual Use of Herbs by S Lavender & A Franklin
In Search of Herne the Hunter by Eric Fitch
Magical Guardians - Exploring the Spirit & Nature of Trees by P. Heselton
Magical Lore of Cats by Marion Davies
Magical Lore of Herbs by Marion Davies
Patchwork of Magic by Julia Day
Psychic Self Defence - Real Solutions by Jan Brodie
Sacred Animals by Gordon MacLellan
Sacred Grove - The Mysteries of the Forest by Yvonne Aburrow
Sacred Geometry by Nigel Pennick
Sacred Lore of Horses The by Marion Davies
Secret Places of the Goddess by Philip Heselton
Talking to the Earth by Gordon Maclellan
Taming the Wolf - Full Moon Meditations by Steve Hounsome
VORTEX - The End of History, by Mary Russell

Capall Bann is owned and run by people actively involved in many of the areas in which we publish. Our list is expanding rapidly so do contact us for details on the latest releases.

Capall Bann Publishing, Freshfields, Chieveley, Berks, RG20 8TF